THE TIMELINE HISTORY OF
U.S. PRESIDENTS
AND
FIRST LADIES

Thunder Bay Press
An imprint of the Advantage Publishers Group
10350 Barnes Canyon Road, San Diego, CA 92121
www.thunderbaybooks.com

ISBN-13: 978-1-59223-992-4
ISBN-10: 1-59223-992-7

Library of Congress Cataloging-in-Publication data available upon request.

Printed and Bound by Imago Publishing, Thailand

1 2 3 4 5 13 12 11 10 09

THE AUTHOR
Barbara Greenman has published several books of American history as director of book development for the Literary Guild and Doubleday Book Clubs (now Bookspan). She edited regular revised editions of *The American Presidents* by David and Robin Whitney; and *First Ladies*, *America's First Ladies*, and *Inside the White House* by Betty Boyd Caroli. Recently she compiled *A Treasury of American Quotations*.

CONSULTING EDITOR: Dee McRea

GRAPHIC DESIGN:
Kelli Allen-Pratt, The Design Lady

Every effort has been made to ensure the accuracy of the information presented in this book. The publisher will not assume liability for damages caused by inaccuracies in the data and makes no warranty whatsoever, expressed or implied. The publisher welcomes comments and corrections from the reader, and will make every effort to incorporate them in future editions.

PICTURE CREDITS
Library of Congress (except as noted)
Harry S. Truman Library: page 17, bottom left; page 34, top; page 52, column 3, top:
Ash Lawn, Highland: page 6, column 4, Elizabeth Monroe.
U.S. Department of the Interior, National Park Service, Adams Historical Site: page 8, column 1, Louisa Adams.
President Benjamin Harrison Home: page 8, column 2, Anna Harrison.
James K. Polk Memorial Association: page 8, column 4, Sarah Polk.
The White House: page 20, column 3; page 22, column 3; page 24, column 3.
John F. Kennedy Library: page 20, column 1, Jacqueline Kennedy; page 35, column 3, top; page 43, column 3, top; page 44; page 52, column 2, bottom.
Bush Presidential Materials Project: page 24, column 1, Barbara Bush; page 38, bottom; page 49, bottom right; page 53, bottom right.
Lyndon Baines Johnson Library: page 19, column 1; page 35, bottom left; page 52, column 3, bottom.
Gerald R. Ford Library: page 36, bottom; page 49, bottom left; page 51, far left; page 53, column 3, middle.
U.S. National Archives: page 5, column 2; page 36, top; page 52, column 2, third from top.
Ronald Reagan Library: page 22, column three, Nancy Reagan; page 37, column 3, bottom; page 41, column 3, bottom; page 45, column 3, bottom; page 49, bottom center; page 51, bottom right; page 53, bottom left.
Carter Library: page 53, bottom second from left.
Dwight D. Eisenhower Library: page 34, column 1, bottom; page 47, column 2; page 52, column 4, bottom.
Clinton Library: page 34, column 2, Hillary Clinton.
U.S. Senate: page 24; column 3, page 39
David Gibbons: pages 4--21, thanks for presidential portraits, George Washington--Ronald Reagan. Clinton Library: if: 31 Hillary Clinton.
The Minnesota Independent: by Nancy Olsen, page 23; column 4, Michelle Obama

REFERENCES
Books
Caroli, Betty Boyd. *Inside the White House*. Garden City, New York: GuildAmerica Books, 1992.
Caroli, Betty Boyd. *First Ladies,* 3rd edition. Garden City, New York: GuildAmerica Books, 2001.
DeGregorio, William A. *The Complete Book of U.S. Presidents*. New York: Random House Value Publishing, 2001.
Garrison, Webb. *A Treasury of White House Tales.* Nashville, Tennessee: Rutledge Hill Press, 2002.
Humes, James. *Which President Killed a Man?* New York: McGraw Hill, 2003.
Rubel, David. *Mr. President.* Alexandria, Virginia: Time-Life Books, 1998.
Whitney, David C. and Robin Vaughn Whitney. *The American Presidents*, 9th edition. Garden City, New York: GuildAmerica Books, 2001.
World Almanac and Book of Facts 2004. New York: World Almanac Books, 2004.
Bill Harris. *The First Ladies Fact Book*, New York, Black Dog & Leventhal, 2005.
Michael Beschloss, ed. *American Heritage Illustrated History of the Presidents*, New York, ibooks, Inc, 2003.

Web sites
www.americanpresident.org
http://ap.grolier.com
www.infoplease.com
www.whitehouse.gov

THE TIMELINE HISTORY OF
U.S. PRESIDENTS
AND
FIRST LADIES

Thunder Bay
P · R · E · S · S
San Diego, California

1 GEORGE WASHINGTON
(1732–99)
President (1789–97)

The son of a moderately successful planter, and great-grandson of an English settler, George Washington trained as a surveyor before taking up a military career. Although he owned thousands of acres, he had to borrow money to attend his own inaugural.

BIOGRAPHY

Date of birth: February 22, 1732
Place of birth: Pope's Creek, Westmoreland County, Virginia
Father: Augustine Washington (1694–1743)
Mother: Mary Ball Washington (1708–89)
Wife: Martha Dandridge Custis (1731–1802)
Children: 2 (stepchildren)
Date of death: December 14, 1799
Place of death: Mount Vernon, Virginia
Burial: Mount Vernon, Virginia
Terms: 2
Dates of inaugurations: April 30, 1789; March 4, 1793
Age at first inauguration: 57
Vice president: John Adams
Secretary of state: Thomas Jefferson, Edmund Randolph, Timothy Pickering
Secretary of treasury: Alexander Hamilton, Oliver Wolcott Jr.

HIGHLIGHTS

1748–49 Worked as a land surveyor after ending his education at age fourteen
1752 Appointed major in Virginia militia
1754 Surrendered Fort Necessity to the French
1755 With Braddock, was defeated at Monongahela River
1759 Married Martha Dandridge Custis
1774 Became a delegate to First Continental Congress, Philadelphia
June 15, 1775 Elected commander in chief of the Continental army
June 17, 1775 Battle of Bunker Hill
July 4, 1776 The Declaration of Independence is adopted at Independence Hall in Philadelphia

August 27, 1776 Defeated at battle of Brooklyn
1776–77 Defeated the British in the battle of Trenton on December 26 and of Princeton on January 3
September 11, 1777 Defeated at Brandywine
October 17, 1777 British defeated at Saratoga
1777–78 Winter at Valley Forge
June 1778 British evacuate Philadelphia with Washington in pursuit
October 19, 1781 British surrender at Yorktown
1787 President of Constitutional Convention
1789–93 First term as president
1792 Established first presidential veto
1793–97 Second term

"To make and sell a little flour annually, to repair houses (going fast to ruin), to build one for the security of my papers of a public nature, and to amuse myself in agricultural and rural pursuits, will constitute employment for the few years I have to remain on this terrestrial globe. If . . . I could now and then meet the friends I esteem, it would fill the measure and add zest to my enjoyments; but, if this ever happens, it must be under my own vine and fig tree."

GEORGE WASHINTON ON HIS RETIREMENT, MAY 1797

Washington arriving in New York City for his inauguration, April 30, 1789.

2 JOHN ADAMS
(1735–1826)
President (1797–1801)

A deep thinker, a man of unshakable integrity and independence of mind, Adams was often a difficult man to get along with.

BIOGRAPHY

Date of birth: October 30, 1735
Place of birth: Braintree (Now Quincy), Massachusetts
Father: John Adams (1691–1761)
Mother: Susanna Boylston Adams (1709–97)
Wife: Abigail Smith (1744–1818)
Children: 5
Date of death: July 4, 1826
Place of death: Quincy, Massachusetts
Burial: United First Parish Church in Quincy, Massachusetts
Terms: 1
Date of inauguration: March 4, 1797
Age at inauguration: 61
Vice president: Thomas Jefferson
Secretary of state: Timothy Pickering, John Marshall
Secretary of treasury: Oliver Wolcott Jr., Samuel Dexter

HIGHLIGHTS

1751 Entered Harvard at age sixteen, began teaching upon graduation
1758 After two years reading law began practicing in Braintree
1764 Married Abigail Smith
1774 Elected to First Continental Congress
1789 Elected vice president
1798 Signed Alien and Sedition Acts

"No man who ever held the office of President would congratulate a friend on obtaining it."

JOHN ADAMS

1789

1801

1789 FIRST U.S. CONGRESS MEETS AT NEW YORK ON MARCH **4.**
1790 FIRST PATENT FOR A MECHANICAL SEWING MACHINE IS ISSUED TO ENGLISHMAN THOMAS SAINT.
1791 THOMAS PAINE PUBLISHES *THE RIGHTS OF MAN.*
1792 THE FIRST STONE OF THE WHITE HOUSE (KNOWN AS THE EXECUTIVE MANSION UNTIL THE TWENTIETH CENTURY) IS LAID.

Napoleon

1793 SAMUEL SLATER BUILDS THE FIRST SUCCESSFUL U.S. TEXTILE MILL IN PAWTUCKET, RHODE ISLAND.
1793 REVOLUTIONARIES IN FRANCE EXECUTE KING LOUIS XVI.
1796 PRESIDENT WASHINGTON DELIVERS HIS FAREWELL ADDRESS ON SEPTEMBER **19.**
1797 ANDRÉ-JACQUES GARNERIN PERFORMS FIRST PARACHUTE DESCENT IN PARIS.

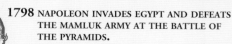

1798 NAPOLEON INVADES EGYPT AND DEFEATS THE MAMLUK ARMY AT THE BATTLE OF THE PYRAMIDS.
1800 FIRST WORKABLE ELECTRIC BATTERY IS PRODUCED BY ITALIAN ALESSANDRO VOLTA.
1800 AMERICAN ROBERT FULTON BUILDS THE FIRST PROPELLER-DRIVEN SUBMARINE.
1800 ON NOVEMBER **1,** JOHN ADAMS IS THE FIRST PRESIDENT TO SLEEP IN THE WHITE HOUSE.

3
THOMAS JEFFERSON
(1743–1826)
President (1801–09)

The American Renaissance man of his age, Jefferson was curious about everything: "There was not a sprig of grass . . . uninteresting to me, nor anything that moves."

BIOGRAPHY
Date of birth: April 13, 1743
Place of birth: Goochland (Albemarle) County, Virginia
Father: Peter Jefferson (1708–57)
Mother: Jane Randolph Jefferson (1720–76)
Wife: Martha Wayles Skelton (1748–82)
Children: 6
Date of death: July 4, 1826
Place of death: Charlottesville, Virginia
Burial: Monticello, Charlottesville, Virginia
Terms: 2
Dates of inaugurations: March 4, 1801; March 4, 1805
Age at first inauguration: 57
Vice president: Aaron Burr, George Clinton
Secretary of state: James Madison
Secretary of treasury: Samuel Dexter, Albert Gallatin

HIGHLIGHTS
1762 Graduated from College of William and Mary in Williamsburg, Virginia
1767 Admitted to the Virginia bar
1769 Elected to the Virginia legislature and began construction of Monticello
January 1, 1772 Married wealthy widow Martha Wayles Skelton
1774 Authored *A Summary View of the Rights of British America*
1776 Drafted the Declaration of Independence
1776–79 Served in the Virginia House of Delegates
1779–81 Governor of Virginia
1782 Death of Martha Jefferson
1783 Elected a delegate of the Continental Congress

1785–89 Minister to France
1790 Became secretary of state in Washington's first administration
1793 Resigned as secretary of state
1796 Lost presidential election to John Adams and became vice president
March 4, 1801 Sworn in as third U.S. president in Washington, D.C.
1803 Purchased Louisiana from France for $15 million at three cents an acre
1804 Won second term as U.S. president
1804 Sent Lewis and Clark on their expedition to the West
1809 Returned to Monticello
1810 Became primary founder of the University of Virginia
July 4, 1826 Died at Monticello

"I know well that no man will ever bring out of that office the reputation which carries him into it. The honeymoon would be as short in that case as in any other; and its moments of ecstasy would be ransomed by years of torment and hatred."
THOMAS JEFFERSON, 1796

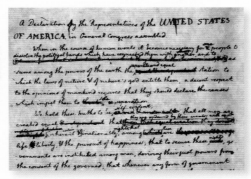

Jefferson's heavily edited draft of the Declaration of Independence.

"I have the consolation . . . of having added nothing to my private fortune during my public service, and of retiring with hands as clean as they are empty."
THOMAS JEFFERSON, MARCH 29, 1807

4
JAMES MADISON
(1751–1836)
President (1809–17)

Although physically unimpressive, James Madison was an intellectual power-house among the founding fathers. John F. Kennedy called him "our most underrated president."

BIOGRAPHY
Date of birth: March 16, 1751
Place of birth: Port Conway, Virginia
Father: James Madison (1723–1801)
Mother: Eleanor Conway Madison (1731–1829)
Wife: Dolley Payne Todd (1768–1849)
Children: None
Date of death: June 28, 1836
Place of death: Montpelier, Virginia
Burial: Montpelier, Virginia
Terms: 2
Dates of inaugurations: March 4, 1809; March 4, 1813
Age at first inauguration: 57
Vice president: George Clinton, Elbridge Gerry
Secretary of state: Robert Smith, James Monroe
Secretary of treasury: Albert Gallatin, George W. Campbell, Alexander J. Dallas

HIGHLIGHTS
1771 Graduated from the College of New Jersey at Princeton
1776 Contributed to the Virginia state constitution
1776–77 Member of Virginia legislature
1780–83 Served as a delegate to Congress
1787–88 Wrote many of *The Federalist* papers
1801–09 Secretary of state under Jefferson
1809–17 Served as the fourth U.S. president
1826 Became rector of University of Virginia

"Justice is the end of government. It ever has been, and ever will be pursued, until it is obtained, or until liberty be lost in the pursuit."
JAMES MADISON

1801

1817

1803 OHIO IS ADMITTED TO STATEHOOD. LOUISIANA IS PURCHASED FROM FRANCE FOR $15 MILLION.
1804 AARON BURR KILLS ALEXANDER HAMILTON IN A DUEL.
1804–06 MERIWETHER LEWIS AND WILLIAM CLARK EXPLORE THE COUNTRY FROM THE MISSISSIPPI RIVER TO THE PACIFIC OCEAN.

1805 U.S. WARSHIPS DEFEAT THE BARBARY PIRATES OF NORTH AFRICA IN THE TRIPOLITANIAN WAR.
1807 BRITISH H.M.S. *LEOPARD* FIRES ON U.S.S. *CHESAPEAKE* CAUSING THE JEFFERSON ADMINISTRATION TO DEMAND AN APOLOGY FROM THE BRITISH GOVERNMENT—A FACTOR LEADING TO WAR IN **1812**.
1811 LONDON BECOMES THE FIRST CITY TO EXCEED **1** MILLION IN POPULATION.

1812 ON JUNE **18**, AMERICA DECLARES WAR ON BRITAIN.
1814 BRITISH CAPTURE AND OCCUPY WASHINGTON, BURNING THE WHITE HOUSE AND OTHER PUBLIC BUILDINGS.
1815 BRITISH ARE DEFEATED BY ANDREW JACKSON AT THE BATTLE OF NEW ORLEANS.
1816 FRENCHMAN RENÉ-THÉOPHILE-HYACINTHE LAENNEC INVENTS THE STETHOSCOPE IN PARIS.

❧ 5 ❧
JAMES MONROE
(1758–1831)
President (1817–25)

The fourth president to have come from Virginia, and the last to have fought in the War of Independence.

BIOGRAPHY
Date of birth: April 28, 1758
Place of birth: Westmoreland County, Virginia
Father: Spence Monroe (d.1744)
Mother: Elizabeth Jones Monroe (dates unknown)
Wife: Elizabeth Kortright (1768–1830)
Children: 3
Date of death: July 4, 1831
Place of death: New York City
Burial: Hollywood Cemetery, Richmond, Virginia
Terms: 2
Dates of inauguration: March 4, 1817; March 5, 1821
Age at first inaugurations: 58
Vice president: Daniel D. Tompkins
Secretary of state: Richard Rush, John Quincy Adams
Secretary of treasury: William H. Crawford

HIGHLIGHTS
1776–80 Fought in War of Independence
1782 Member of Virginia Assembly
February 16, 1786 Married Elizabeth Kortright
1790–94 Served as U.S senator for Virginia
1794–96 Minister to France
1799–1802 Served as governor of Virginia
1803–07 Minister to Britain
1811–17 Secretary of state under Madison
1814–15 Secretary of war under Madison
1817–25 Served as fifth U.S. president

❧ 6 ❧
JOHN QUINCY ADAMS
(1767–1848)
President (1825–29)

The first son of a president to become president himself, John Quincy Adams had an unhappy four years in the White House.

BIOGRAPHY
Date of birth: July 11, 1767
Place of birth: Quincy, Massachusetts
Father: John Adams (1735–1826)
Mother: Abigail Smith Adams (1744–1818)
Wife: Louisa Catherine Johnson (1775–1852)
Children: 4
Date of death: February 23, 1848
Place of death: Washington, D.C.
Burial: United First Parish Church, Quincy, Massachusetts
Terms: 1
Date of inauguration: March 4, 1825
Age at inauguration: 57
Vice president: John C. Calhoun
Secretary of state: Henry Clay
Secretary of treasury: Richard Rush

HIGHLIGHTS
1751 Entered Harvard at age sixteen, began teaching upon graduation
1758 After two years reading law, began practicing in Braintree
1764 Married Abigail Smith
1770 Elected to Massachusetts General Court
1770 Defended British soldiers charged in Boston Massacre
1773 Nominated for Governor's Council; vetoed by royal governor
1774 Elected to First Continental Congress
1778 Appointed member of Commission to France
1789 Elected vice president
1796 Elected president
1798 Signed Alien and Sedition Acts

❧ 7 ❧
ANDREW JACKSON
(1767–1845)
President (1829–37)

The first president to come from poverty, "Old Hickory" made his reputation as a tough Indian fighter and fearless duelist.

BIOGRAPHY
Date of birth: March 15, 1767
Place of birth: The Waxhaws, in the Piedmont region of North and South Carolina
Father: Andrew Jackson (d.1767)
Mother: Elizabeth Hutchinson Jackson (d.1781)
Wife: Rachel Donelson Robards (1767–1828)
Children: 1
Date of death: June 8, 1845
Place of death: Nashville, Tennessee
Burial: The Hermitage, Nashville, Tennessee
Terms: 2
Dates of inaugurations: March 4, 1829; March 4, 1833
Age at first inauguration: 61
Vice president: John C. Calhoun, Martin Van Buren
Secretary of state: Martin Van Buren, Edward Livingston, Louis McLane, John Forsyth
Secretary of treasury: Samuel D. Ingham, Louis McLane, William J. Duane, Roger B. Taney, Levi Woodbury

HIGHLIGHTS
1791 Married Rachel Donelson Robards, but discovered her divorce was not final and remarried in 1794
1780 Joined Continental army at age thirteen, was taken prisoner but exchanged after about two weeks
1818 Invaded Florida, overthrew Spanish governor
1823 Elected U.S. senator
1828 Elected president

1817

1829

1829

1817 MISSISSIPPI IS ADMITTED TO STATEHOOD.

1817–18 ANDREW JACKSON INVADES FLORIDA DURING THE SEMINOLE WARS.

1818 CONVENTION OF **1818** BETWEEN GREAT BRITAIN AND UNITED STATES SETTLES BORDER BETWEEN UNITED STATES AND CANADA.

1819 ALABAMA IS ADMITTED TO STATEHOOD.

1820 FIRST NATURAL GAS STREET LIGHTING IN THE UNITED STATES AT FREDONIA IN NEW YORK.

1823 ON DECEMBER 2, THE MONROE DOCTRINE IS DECLARED: NO EUROPEAN POWER TO BE ABLE TO COLONIZE ANY PART OF THE AMERICAN CONTINENT.

1825 ERIE CANAL, BEGUN IN **1817**, IS COMPLETED AND OPENS UP SETTLEMENT OF THE WEST.

1826 FRENCH PHYSICIST JOSEPH NIÉPCE MAKES THE FIRST PHOTOGRAPH.

1828 FIRST PUBLIC RAILROAD IN THE UNITED STATES BEGINS CONSTRUCTION IN BALTIMORE AND OHIO.

1830 THE MORMON CHURCH IS FOUNDED BY JOSEPH SMITH IN FAYETTE, NEW YORK.

1832 NEW ENGLAND ANTISLAVERY SOCIETY IS ESTABLISHED, FOLLOWED IN **1833** BY AMERICAN ANTISLAVERY SOCIETY.

1835 SAMUEL MORSE PROVES SIGNALS COULD BE TRANSMITTED BY WIRE.

Joseph Smith

❧ 8 ❧
MARTIN VAN BUREN
(1782–1862)
President (1837–41)

The first president to have been born an American citizen, Martin Van Buren was also the first to use "modern" political methods based on the party machine.

BIOGRAPHY
Date of birth: December 5, 1782
Place of birth: Kinderhook, New York
Father: Abraham Van Buren (1737–1817)
Mother: Maria Hoes Van Alen Van Buren (1747–1818)
Wife: Hannah Hoes (1783–1819)
Children: 4
Date of death: July 24, 1862
Place of death: Kinderhook, New York
Burial: Kinderhook, New York
Terms: 1
Date of inauguration: March 4, 1837
Age at inauguration: 54
Vice president: Richard M. Johnson
Secretary of state: John Forsyth
Secretary of treasury: Levi Woodbury

HIGHLIGHTS
1800 Campaigned for Thomas Jefferson
1803 Admitted to New York bar
1807 Married childhood sweetheart Hannah Hoes
1821 Elected U.S. senator
1828 Elected governor of New York
1829–31 U.S. secretary of state
1832 Elected vice president
1836 Elected president
1836 Opposed admission of Texas because of tensions over slavery; Texas finally became a state in 1845
1837 Two months after inauguration, several banks stopped converting paper money into silver and gold and set off nationwide panic leading to depression

❧ 9 ❧
WILLIAM HENRY HARRISON
(1773–1841)
President (1841)

The first president to die in office, one month after his inauguration, Harrison was a candidate of the new Whig Party and won the election against the incumbent Van Buren.

BIOGRAPHY
Date of birth: February 9, 1773
Place of birth: Berkeley Plantation, Charles City County, Virginia
Father: Benjamin Harrison (1726–91)
Mother: Elizabeth Bassett Harrison (1730–92)
Wife: Anna Tuthill Symmes (1775–1864)
Children: 10
Date of death: April 4, 1841
Place of death: Washington, D.C.
Burial: North Bend, Ohio
Terms: 1 (incomplete)
Date of inauguration: March 4, 1841
Age at inauguration: 68
Vice president: John Tyler
Secretary of state: Daniel Webster
Secretary of treasury: Thomas Ewing

HIGHLIGHTS
1791 Began study of medicine under Dr. Benjamin Rush before dropping out to join the army
1795 Married Anna Tuthill Symmes
1799 Elected Northwest Territory delegate to U.S. House of Representatives
1813 Led force of 2,400 volunteers to victory against British at battle of the Thames near Chatham, Ontario
1816 Elected U.S. representative
1825–1828 U.S. senator
1840 Elected president
1841 Died of pneumonia

"The only legitimate right to govern is an express grant of power from the governed."
WILLIAM HENRY HARRISON

❧ 10 ❧
JOHN TYLER
(1790–1862)
President (1841–45)

At Harrison's death, John Tyler became the nation's first vice president to become president by an "act of God."

BIOGRAPHY
Date of birth: March 29, 1790
Place of birth: Greenway Plantation, Charles City County, Virginia
Father: John Tyler (1747–1813)
Mother: Mary Armistead Tyler (1761–97)
Wife: (1) Letitia Christian (1790–1842); (2) Julia Gardiner (1820–89)
Children: (1) 8; (2) 7
Date of death: January 18, 1862
Place of death: Richmond, Virginia
Burial: Richmond, Virginia
Terms: 1 (partial)
Date of inauguration: April 6, 1841
Age at inauguration: 51
Vice president: None
Secretary of state: Daniel Webster, Abel P. Upshur, John C. Calhoun
Secretary of treasury: Thomas Ewing, Walter Forward, John C. Spencer, George M. Bibb

HIGHLIGHTS
1809 Admitted to Virginia bar
1813 Married Letitia Christian, who died in 1842
1816 Elected U.S. representative for Richmond district of Virginia
1825–27 Governor of Virginia
1827–36 U.S. senator
1840 Elected vice president
April 6, 1841 Sworn in as president two days after Harrison's death
1841 Signed law recognizing right of purchase by those who settled on and improved 160 acres of public land
1844 Married Julia Gardiner
1845 Approved annexation of Texas
1845 Florida admitted to Union

1837

1845

1839 WILLIAM TALBOT ANNOUNCES HIS INVENTION OF THE NEGATIVE-POSITIVE PROCESS, LAYING BASE FOR MODERN PHOTOGRAPHY.

1841 EDGAR ALLAN POE PUBLISHES THE "THE MURDERS IN THE RUE MORGUE," CALLED THE FIRST AMERICAN DETECTIVE STORY.

1842 ETHER IS FIRST USED AS AN ANESTHETIC, BY A TWENTY-SEVEN-YEAR-OLD GEORGIA PHYSICIAN, DR. CRAWFORD WILLIAMSON LONG.

1843 THE "GREAT MIGRATION" OF NEARLY **1,000** PIONEERS SETS OUT BY WAGON TRAIN ON THE OREGON TRAIL, BEGINNING A MASSIVE WESTWARD MOVEMENT.

1844 INVENTOR SAMUEL MORSE SENDS THE FIRST MESSAGE OVER THE FIRST TELEGRAPH LINE, FROM BALTIMORE, MARYLAND, TO WASHINGTON, D.C.

1845 TEXAS IS ADMITTED TO THE UNION.

1845–82 THE GREAT FAMINE REDUCES THE POPULATION OF IRELAND BY NEARLY **25** PERCENT.

❧ 11 ❧
JAMES KNOX POLK
(1795–1849)
President (1845–49)

A supporter of "manifest destiny," a belief that the nation should rule across the whole North American continent, Polk increased the size of the country more than any other president since Jefferson. In one term he accomplished all four goals he had set in his campaign.

BIOGRAPHY
Date of birth: November 2, 1795
Place of birth: Pineville, North Carolina
Father: Samuel Polk (1772–1827)
Mother: Jane Knox Polk (1776–1852)
Wife: Sarah Childress (1803–91)
Children: None
Date of death: June 15, 1849
Place of death: Nashville, Tennessee
Burial: Nashville, Tennessee
Terms: 1
Date of inauguration: March 4, 1845
Age at inauguration: 49
Vice president: George M. Dallas
Secretary of state: James Buchanan
Secretary of treasury: Robert J. Walker

HIGHLIGHTS
1818 Graduated from the University of North Carolina
1820 Admitted to the Tennessee bar
1823–25 Elected to state legislature of Tennessee
January 1, 1824 Married Sarah Childress
1825–39 U.S. representative from Tennessee
1835–39 Speaker of the House of Representatives
1839–41 Governor of Tennessee
1845–49 President of the United States
1846 Walker Tariff, reducing tax on imports
1846 Independent Treasury Act
1846 Oregon Treaty, settling boundary dispute
1846–48 Mexican War; Mexico ceded to U.S. all or part of California, Nevada, Utah, Wyoming, Colorado, Texas, New Mexico, and Arizona

❧ 12 ❧
ZACHARY TAYLOR
(1784–1850)
President (1849–50)

A national hero after victory in the Mexican War (1847), Taylor won election with no previous political experience. Although a slaveholder, he opposed the right of secession.

BIOGRAPHY
Date of birth: November 24, 1784
Place of birth: Orange County, Virginia
Father: Richard Taylor (1744–1829)
Mother: Sarah Strother Taylor (1760–1822)
Wife: Margaret Mackall Smith (1788–1852)
Children: 6
Date of death: July 9, 1850
Place of death: Washington, D.C.
Burial: Louisville, Kentucky
Terms: 1 (incomplete)
Date of inauguration: March 5, 1849
Age at inauguration: 64
Vice president: Millard Fillmore
Secretary of state: John M. Clayton
Secretary of treasury: W. M. Meredith

HIGHLIGHTS
1808 Commissioned first lieutenant
1810 Promoted to captain
June 21, 1810 Married Margaret Mackall Smith
January 1815 Promoted to major but reduced to captain in demobilization after War of 1812; in June he resigned his commission
1816 Rejoined army as a major
1846 Promoted to major general early in Mexican War
1847 Defeated Santa Anna and became national hero known as "Old Rough and Ready"
1848 Elected president
1850 Clayton-Bulwer Treaty with Great Britain stipulated that any canal across Central America would be neutral
1850 Died in office

❧ 13 ❧
MILLARD FILLMORE
(1800–74)
President (1850–53)

Becoming president on the death of Zachary Taylor, Fillmore supported the Compromise of 1850 as a "final settlement" of the differences between the North and South.

BIOGRAPHY
Date of birth: January 7, 1800
Place of birth: Locke, New York
Father: Nathaniel Fillmore (1771–1863)
Mother: Phoebe Millard Fillmore (1780–1831)
Wife: (1) Abigail Powers (1798–1853); (2) Caroline McIntosh (1813–81)
Children: (1) 2
Date of death: March 8, 1874
Place of death: Buffalo, New York
Burial: Buffalo, New York
Terms: 1 (partial)
Date of inauguration: July 10, 1850
Age at inauguration: 50
Vice president: None
Secretary of state: Daniel Webster, Edward Everett
Secretary of treasury: Thomas Corwin

HIGHLIGHTS
1823 Admitted to the New York bar
1829–31 New York state assemblyman
1833–35 and 1837–43 U.S. representative
1848 Elected vice president
July 10, 1850 Sworn in as president one day after the death of President Zachary Taylor
1850 Signed into law the Compromise of 1850, which admitted California as a free state, defined Texas's borders, established the territories of New Mexico and Utah, ended slave trading in Washington, D.C., and enacted the Fugitive Slave Act
1852 Sent Commodore Matthew C. Perry on a mission to get Japan to open at least one port to trade and grant other concessions

---

1845

1850

1850

1846 ELIAS HOWE INVENTS THE FIRST SUCCESSFUL SEWING MACHINE.

1846–48 U.S.-MEXICAN WAR. MEXICO CEDES TEXAS, CALIFORNIA, AND OTHER TERRITORY.

1847 FIRST OFFICIALLY ISSUED U.S. POSTAGE STAMPS GO ON SALE

1848 GOLD IS DISCOVERED IN CALIFORNIA.

1849 A STEAMBOAT IN ST. LOUIS CATCHES FIRE AND NEARLY BURNS DOWN THE ENTIRE CITY.

1849 THE FIRST SEGMENT OF THE PENNSYLVANIA RAILROAD OPENS FOR SERVICE.

1850 NATIONAL WOMEN'S RIGHTS CONVENTION MEETS IN WORCESTER, MASSACHUSETTS.

1850 AMERICAN EXPRESS IS FOUNDED BY HENRY WELLS AND WILLIAM FARGO.

1852 *UNCLE TOM'S CABIN* BY HARRIET BEECHER STOWE IS PUBLISHED.

Prospectors

1852 FREDERICK DOUGLASS DELIVERS HIS FAMOUS SPEECH, "THE MEANING OF JULY 4TH FOR THE NEGRO."

≈ 14 ≈
FRANKLIN PIERCE
(1804–69)
President (1853–57)

Handsome and congenial, Pierce is the only president who served a complete term without making a single change in his cabinet. Although against slavery, Pierce was damaged by the Kansas-Nebraska disaster and lost the nomination in 1856.

BIOGRAPHY
Date of birth: November 23, 1804
Place of birth: Hillsboro, New Hampshire
Father: Benjamin Pierce (1757–1839)
Mother: Anna Kendrick Pierce (1768–1838)
Wife: Jane Means Appleton (1806–63)
Children: 3
Date of death: October 8, 1869
Place of death: Concord, New Hampshire
Burial: Concord, New Hampshire
Terms: 1
Date of inauguration: March 4, 1853
Age at inauguration: 48
Vice president: William R. D. King
Secretary of state: William L. Marcy
Secretary of treasury: James Guthrie

HIGHLIGHTS
1827 Admitted to the bar
1833–37 U.S. representative
1834 Married Jane Means Appleton
1837–42 U.S. senator
1852 Elected president
1856 John Brown led antislavery raid at Pottawatomie Creek in which five proslavery men died

". . . it would ruin a noble character (though one of limited scope) for him to admit any idea that were not entertained by the fathers of the Constitution and the Republic . . ."

NATHANIEL HAWTHORNE ON FRANKLIN PIERCE

≈ 15 ≈
JAMES BUCHANAN
(1791–1868)
President (1857–61)

The only president who never married, Buchanan presided over a nation rapidly dividing because of slavery. Seven states withdrew from the Union during his administration.

BIOGRAPHY
Date of birth: April 23, 1791
Place of birth: Near Mercersburg, Pennsylvania
Father: James Buchanan Sr. (1761–1821)
Mother: Elizabeth Speer Buchanan (1767–1833)
Wife: None
Children: None
Date of death: June 1, 1868
Place of death: Wheatland, near Lancaster, Pennsylvania
Burial: Woodward Cemetery, near Lancaster, Pennsylvania
Terms: 1
Date of inauguration: March 4, 1857
Age at inauguration: 65
Vice president: John C. Breckinridge
Secretary of state: Lewis Cass, Jeremiah S. Black
Secretary of treasury: Howell Cobb, Philip F. Thomas, John A. Dix

HIGHLIGHTS
1812 Admitted to the bar
1819 Quarreled with fiancé Anne Coleman, who broke off engagement and died a few months later; Buchanan never married
1856 Elected president
1857 Supreme Court ruled that a slave did not become a free citizen by traveling north of the Missouri Compromise line
1858 Minnesota admitted to the Union
1859 Oregon admitted to the Union
1860 After Abraham Lincoln's election, seven Southern states form Confederate States of America
1861 Kansas admitted to the Union

≈ 16 ≈
ABRAHAM LINCOLN
(1809–65)
President (1861–65)

Unpretentious, plain-spoken, with a ready wit, Lincoln had a dark side and wrestled with severe bouts of depression. He estimated he had about one year of formal education and a childhood that "can be condensed into a single sentence: The short and simple annals of the poor."

BIOGRAPHY
Date of birth: February 12, 1809
Place of birth: Hardin (now Larue) County, Kentucky
Father: Thomas Lincoln (1778–1851)
Mother: Nancy Hanks Lincoln (1784–1818)
Wife: Mary Todd (1818–82)
Children: 4
Date of death: April 15, 1865
Place of death: Washington, D.C.
Burial: Springfield, Illinois
Terms: 2 (second incomplete)
Dates of inaugurations: March 4, 1861; March 4, 1865
Age at first inauguration: 52
Vice president: Hannibal Hamlin, Andrew Johnson
Secretary of state: William H. Seward
Secretary of treasury: Salmon P. Chase, William P. Fessenden, Hugh McCulloch

HIGHLIGHTS
1832 Served as a captain in the Black Hawk War
1833–36 Appointed postmaster of New Salem, Illinois
1834–42 Elected to Illinois legislature
1836 Licensed to practice law
November 4, 1842 Married Mary Todd
1846 Elected to Congress as representative from Illinois
1858 Campaigned unsuccessfully for U.S. Senate; debated slavery issue with Stephen Douglas
1860 Elected president
April 12, 1861 Confederates take Fort Sumter; Civil War begins

1853

1865

1853 ELISHA OTIS BUILDS FIRST SAFETY ELEVATOR.

1853 LEVI STRAUSS SAILS TO SAN FRANCISCO; MAKES DURABLE PANTS CALLED JEANS FOR GOLD MINERS.

1853 ABBA ALCOTT AND SEVENTY-THREE OTHER WOMEN PETITION MASSACHUSETTS CONSTITUTIONAL CONVENTION URGING SUFFRAGE FOR WOMEN.

1861 WESTERN UNION COMPLETES FIRST TRANSCONTINENTAL TELEGRAPH LINE.

1861 SEVEN SOUTHERN STATES FORM CONFEDERATE STATES OF AMERICA.

1861 HENRY WADSWORTH LONGFELLOW WRITES "PAUL REVERE'S RIDE."

1862 BATTLE OF ANTIETAM, THE BLOODIEST ONE-DAY BATTLE OF THE CIVIL WAR, OCCURS ON SEPTEMBER 17.

1863 LINCOLN DECLARES THANKSGIVING DAY AN OFFICIAL NATIONAL HOLIDAY.

1865 ACCORDING TO LEGEND, JOHN STETSON INVENTS THE FAMOUS COWBOY HAT WHILE ON AN UNSUCCESSFUL GOLD PROSPECTING TRIP TO COLORADO.

September 1862 Issued the
Emancipation Proclamation
November 19, 1863 Delivered
Gettysburg Address
1864 Won reelection to a second term
April 9, 1865 Lee's surrender to
Grant at Appomattox, Virginia
April 14, 1865 Wounded by assassin
John Wilkes Booth while at Ford's
Theatre to see the comedy *Our
American Cousin*.
April 15, 1865 Died in Washington, D.C.

*"If any personal description
of me is thought desirable . . .
I am, in height, six feet, four
inches, nearly; lean in flesh,
weighing, on an average, one
hundred and eighty pounds;
dark complexion, with coarse
black hair and grey eyes . . ."*

ABRAHAM LINCOLN, 1859

Lincoln's second inauguration

*"Four score and seven years ago,
our fathers brought forth on this
continent a new nation, conceived
in liberty, and dedicated to the
proposition that all men are
created equal."*

ABRAHAM LINCOLN, THE GETTYSBURG ADDRESS, 1863

✺ 17 ✺
ANDREW JOHNSON
(1808–75)
President (1865–69)

*A defender of the rights
of the working man
and loyal to the Union,
Johnson presided over
the bitterly divisive
"reconstruction" of the
former Confederate
states and, in 1867,
the purchase of Alaska.
Johnson was impeached,
but acquitted, over
his dismissal of the
secretary of war.*

BIOGRAPHY
Date of birth: December 29, 1808
Place of birth: Raleigh, North Carolina
Father: Jacob Johnson (1778–1812)
Mother: Mary McDonough Johnson
(1783–1856)
Wife: Eliza McCardle (1810–76)
Children: 5
Date of death: July 31, 1875
Place of death: Carter Station, Tennessee
Burial: Greeneville, Tennessee
Terms: 1
Date of inauguration: April 15, 1865
Age at inauguration: 56
Vice president: None
Secretary of state: William H. Seward
Secretary of treasury: Hugh McCulloch

HIGHLIGHTS
1843–51 U.S. representative
1853–57 Governor of Tennessee
1857–62 U.S. senator
1862 Appointed military governor of
Tennessee with rank of brigadier general
1864 Elected vice president
April 15, 1865 Sworn in as president
within hours of Abraham Lincoln's death
1865 Thirteenth Amendment ratified,
outlawing slavery and involuntary servitude
1867 United States purchased Alaska
from Russia for $7.2 million
1867 Nebraska admitted to Union
1868 Fourteenth Amendment,
guaranteeing due process of law, ratified
1868 Impeached on charges of violating
Tenure of Office Act; acquitted in
New Salem, Illinois

✺ 18 ✺
ULYSSES S. GRANT
(1822–85)
President (1869–77)

*A graduate of West
Point and a professional
soldier, Grant served in
the Mexican War and
the Civil War, rising to
General of the Army,
the first commander
since Washington to
hold that rank. Grant
was the first president
whose administration
was marked by
major scandals.*

BIOGRAPHY
Date of birth: April 27, 1822
Place of birth: Point Pleasant, Ohio
Father: Jesse Root Grant (1794–1873)
Mother: Hannah Simpson Grant (1798–1883)
Wife: Julia Dent (1826–1902)
Children: 4
Date of death: July 23, 1885
Place of death: Mount McGregor, New York
Burial: Grant's Tomb, New York City
Terms: 2
Dates of inaugurations: March 4, 1869;
March 4, 1873
Age at first inauguration: 46
Vice president: Schuyler Colfax,
Henry Wilson
Secretary of state: Elihu B. Washbourne,
Hamilton Fish
Secretary of treasury: George S. Boutwell,
William A. Richardson

HIGHLIGHTS
1843 Graduated from West Point
1846–48 Served in the Mexican War
August 22, 1848 Married Julia Dent
1861 Joined the Union army, rising to rank
of lieutenant general
April 9, 1865 Accepted Lee's surrender at
Appomattox, Virginia
1868 Elected president under campaign
slogan "Let us have peace."
1869–77 Administrations marked by
major scandals
1870 Fifteenth Amendment ratified,
outlawing discrimination in voting rights
due to race, color, or previous servitude
September 1873 Panic of 1873 leading
to five-year depression

1865

1869

1869

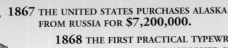

1867 THE UNITED STATES PURCHASES ALASKA
FROM RUSSIA FOR **$7,200,000.**

1868 THE FIRST PRACTICAL TYPEWRITER IS
PATENTED BY CHRISTOPHER SHOLES.

1868 LOUISA MAY ALCOTT PUBLISHES
LITTLE WOMEN.

1869 THE FIRST TRANSCONTINENTAL
RAILROAD LINE IS COMPLETED
AT PROMONTORY, UTAH.

1869 THE FIRST COLLEGE
FOOTBALL GAME IS PLAYED:
RUTGERS V. PRINCETON.

1871 THE GREAT CHICAGO FIRE KILLS HUNDREDS
AND DESTROYS FOUR SQUARE MILES.

1872 ON MARCH **1**, CONGRESS SETS
ASIDE **3,468** SQUARE MILES FOR
YELLOWSTONE NATIONAL PARK,
WHICH INCLUDES LAKES, CANYONS,
A RIVER, AND MOUNTAIN RANGES.

1876 ALEXANDER GRAHAM BELL
PATENTS THE TELEPHONE.

❧ 19 ❧
RUTHERFORD B. HAYES
(1822–93)
President (1877–81)

A Civil War major and governor of Ohio, Hayes ran for president against the Democrat Samuel J. Tilden. Tilden won the popular vote, but the voting was disputed and Hayes won by a margin of one electoral vote.

BIOGRAPHY
Date of birth: October 4, 1822
Place of birth: Delaware, Ohio
Father: Rutherford Hayes (1787–1822)
Mother: Sophia Birchard Hayes (1792–1866)
Wife: Lucy Ware Webb (1831–89)
Children: 8
Date of death: January 17, 1893
Place of death: Fremont, Ohio
Burial: Fremont, Ohio
Terms: 1
Date of inauguration: March 5, 1877
Age at inauguration: 54
Vice president: William A. Wheeler
Secretary of state: William M. Evarts
Secretary of treasury: John Sherman

HIGHLIGHTS
1842 Graduated from Kenyon College and began studying law
1843 Entered Harvard Law School
1845 Graduated from law school; admitted to Ohio bar
December 30, 1852 Married Lucy Ware Webb
1858–61 Cincinnati city solicitor
1861 Joined Twenty-third Ohio Volunteer Infantry Regiment
1861 Appointed judge advocate general of Ohio Department
March 1865 Breveted major general of volunteers; June, resigned from army
1868–72 and 1876–77 Governor of Ohio
1876 Elected president
1877 Withdrew last Union troops from South
1877 Proposed civil service reform

❧ 20 ❧
JAMES A. GARFIELD
(1831–81)
President (1881)

The last president born in a log cabin, he became a major general in the Union army. He was assassinated on his way to his college reunion, where he was to receive an honorary degree.

BIOGRAPHY
Date of birth: November 19, 1831
Place of birth: Orange, Ohio
Father: Abram Garfield (1799–1833)
Mother: Eliza Ballou Garfield (1801–88)
Wife: Lucretia Rudolph (1832–1918)
Children: 7
Date of death: September 19, 1881
Place of death: Elberon, New Jersey
Burial: Cleveland, Ohio
Terms: 1 (incomplete)
Date of inauguration: March 4, 1881
Age at inauguration: 49
Vice president: Chester A. Arthur
Secretary of state: James G. Blaine
Secretary of treasury: William Windom

HIGHLIGHTS
1831 Born in log cabin built by his father
1856 Graduated with honors from Williams College
1856–57 Instructor in Classical Languages, Eclectic Institute in Ohio
1857–61 President of Eclectic Institute
1858 Married Lucretia Rudolph
1859–61 Ohio state senator
1863 Brigadier General Garfield appointed chief of staff under Major General William S. Rosencrans
1863–80 U.S. representative
1880 Elected president
1881 Ordered investigation of irregularities in awarding of mail route contracts
July 2, 1881 Shot by Charles J. Guiteau, disappointed over being turned down for a job; died two and a half months later on September 19

❧ 21 ❧
CHESTER A. ARTHUR
(1829–86)
President (1881–85)

Arthur, a lawyer by training, and known as the "gentleman boss" of the Republican Party in New York City, was an organizational rather than inspirational politician.

BIOGRAPHY
Date of birth: October 5, 1829
Place of birth: North Fairfield, Vermont
Father: Reverend William Arthur (1796–1875)
Mother: Malvina Stone Arthur (1802–69)
Wife: Ellen Lewis Herndon (1837–80)
Children: 3
Date of death: November 18, 1886
Place of death: New York City
Burial: Albany, New York
Terms: 1 (partial)
Age at inauguration: 51
Date of inauguration: September 20, 1881
Vice president: None
Secretary of state: James G. Blaine, Frederick T. Frelinghuysen
Secretary of treasury: William Windom, Charles J. Folger, Walter Q. Gresham, Hugh McCulloch

HIGHLIGHTS
1848 Graduated in top third of class at Union College, member of Phi Beta Kappa, began studying law
1854 Admitted to the bar
1859 Married Ellen Lewis Herndon
1871–78 Collector of Port of New York
1880 Elected vice president
September 20, 1881 Sworn in as president at 2:15 a.m.
1882 Chinese Exclusion Act suspended Chinese immigration for ten years
1883 Pendleton Act
1883 Created the modern civil service

1877

1885

1877 THOMAS EDISON INVENTS THE PHONOGRAPH.

1879 FRANK W. WOOLWORTH OPENS THE GREAT FIVE-CENT STORE IN UTICA, NEW YORK.

1879 SALOON OWNER JAMES RITTY PATENTS THE CASH REGISTER, CALLED THE "INCORRUPTIBLE CASHIER."

1881 NURSE CLARA BARTON FOUNDS THE AMERICAN RED CROSS.

1882 ALL CHINESE IMMIGRANT LABORERS ARE DENIED ACCESS TO THE UNITED STATES DURING THE CHINESE EXCLUSION ACT.

Clara Barton

1883 AMERICAN AND CANADIAN RAILROAD COMPANIES ADOPT THE FOUR TRANSCONTINENTAL TIME ZONES THAT WE USE TODAY.

1883 BUFFALO BILL CODY'S WILD WEST SHOW OPENS IN OMAHA, NEBRASKA, BEGINNING A THIRTY-YEAR RUN.

1883 SCOTTISH AUTHOR ROBERT LOUIS STEVENSON PUBLISHES *TREASURE ISLAND*.

Buffalo Bill

⚶ 22 & 24 ⚶
GROVER CLEVELAND
(1837–1908)
President (1885–89; 1893–97)

Cleveland is the only president to serve two nonconsecutive terms, and to be married in the White House. After four prosperous years of his first term, his second term began with a severe economic depression—the Panic of 1893.

BIOGRAPHY
Date of birth: March 18, 1837
Place of birth: Caldwell, New Jersey
Father: Reverend Richard Cleveland (1804–53)
Mother: Ann Neal Cleveland (1806–82)
Wife: Frances Folsom (1864–1947)
Children: 5
Date of death: June 24, 1908
Place of death: Princeton, New Jersey
Burial: Princeton, New Jersey
Terms: 2
Dates of inaugurations: March 4, 1885; March 4, 1893
Age at first inauguration: 47
Vice president: Thomas A. Hendricks, Adlai E. Stevenson
Secretary of state: Thomas F. Bayard, Walter Q. Gresham, Richard Olney
Secretary of treasury: Daniel Manning, Charles S. Fairchild, John G. Carlisle

HIGHLIGHTS
1859 Admitted to the bar to practice law
1871–73 Served as sheriff of Erie County, New York
1883 Elected governor of New York
1884 Elected twenty-second president
June 2, 1886 Married Frances Folsom at the White House
1889–93 Practiced law in New York City
1892 Elected twenty-fourth president
1893 In second administration, failure of Philadelphia and Reading Railroad in February set off a financial panic that led to a four-year depression
1896 Utah admitted to Union
1901 Trustee of Princeton University

⚶ 23 ⚶
BENJAMIN HARRISON
(1833–1901)
President (1889–93)

A grandson of President William Henry Harrison, a soldier, lawyer, and senator from Indiana, Harrison saw the continuing growth of the nation with six new states admitted during his term. By 1890 the country was settled from coast to coast.

BIOGRAPHY
Date of birth: August 20, 1833
Place of birth: North Bend, Ohio
Father: John Scott Harrison (1804–78)
Mother: Elizabeth Irwin Harrison (1810–1950)
Wife: (1) Caroline Lavinia Scott (1832–92); (2) Mary Scott Dimmick (1858–1948)
Children: (1) 2; (2) 1
Date of death: March 13, 1901
Place of death: Indianapolis, Indiana
Burial: Indianapolis, Indiana
Terms: 1
Date of inauguration: March 4, 1889
Age at inauguration: 55
Vice president: Levi P. Morton
Secretary of state: James G. Blaine, John W. Foster
Secretary of treasury: William Windom, Charles Foster

HIGHLIGHTS
1853 Married Caroline Lavinia Scott, who died in 1892
1854 Admitted to the bar
1857 Elected Indianapolis city attorney
1862–65 Served with Seventieth Indiana Infantry Regiment
1881–87 U.S. senator
1888 Elected president
1889 North Dakota, South Dakota, Montana, Washington admitted to Union
1890 Sherman Anti-Trust Act was first of laws attempting to break power of monopolies
1890 Idaho and Wyoming admitted to Union
1896 Married Mary Scott Dimmick

⚶ 25 ⚶
WILLIAM McKINLEY
(1843–1901)
President (1897–1901)

Although a conciliator by nature, McKinley was drawn into war with Spain over Cuba. He was assassinated shortly after the start of his second term.

BIOGRAPHY
Date of birth: January 29, 1843
Place of birth: Niles, Ohio
Father: William McKinley Sr. (1807–92)
Mother: Nancy Allison McKinley (1809–97)
Wife: Ida Saxton (1847–1907)
Children: 2
Date of death: September 14, 1901
Place of death: Buffalo, New York
Burial: Canton, Ohio
Terms: 2 (second incomplete)
Dates of inaugurations: March 4, 1897; March 4, 1901
Age at first inauguration: 54
Vice president: Garret A. Hobart, Theodore Roosevelt
Secretary of state: John Sherman, William R. Day, John M. Hay
Secretary of treasury: Lyman J. Gage

HIGHLIGHTS
1866–67 Attended Albany Law School in New York, but dropped out without graduating
1867 Admitted to the bar
1869 Elected Stark County prosecutor
1871 Married Ida Saxton
1877–83 and 1885–91 U.S. representative
1892–96 Governor of Ohio
1896 Elected president
July 1898 Signed joint congressional resolution annexing Hawaiian Islands
September 6, 1901 Shot by Leon Czolgosz, an unemployed wire mill worker

---

1885

1885 THE AMERICAN EDITION OF MARK TWAIN'S *THE ADVENTURES OF HUCKLEBERRY FINN* IS PUBLISHED.

1885 THE FIRST PETROL-POWERED AUTOMOBILE (A THREE-WHEELER) IS BUILT IN GERMANY BY KARL BENZ.

1885 BRITISH GENERAL GORDON AND HIS FORCE ARE MASSACRED AT KHARTOUM, SUDAN, BY TROOPS OF THE MAHDI.

1885 CHICAGO'S HOME INSURANCE BUILDING, THE WORLD'S FIRST SKYSCRAPER, IS COMPLETED.

1886 ON OCTOBER **26**, THE STATUE OF LIBERTY, A GIFT FROM FRANCE, IS INAUGURATED.

1887 ON MAY **8**, COCA-COLA IS FIRST SOLD AT JACOB'S PHARMACY IN ATLANTA, GEORGIA.

1892 ELLIS ISLAND IS OPENED TO IMMIGRANTS.

Statue of Liberty

1893

1897

1893 THE DURYEA BROTHERS TEST THEIR "GASOLINE BUGGY," THE FIRST AMERICAN-BUILT GASOLINE-POWERED AUTOMOBILE.

1893 MILTON HERSHEY BUYS CHOCOLATE-MAKING EQUIPMENT AT WORLD'S COLUMBIAN EXPOSITION AND BEGINS THE VENTURE THAT BECOMES THE HERSHEY CHOCOLATE COMPANY IN **1905**.

1897 FIRST U.S. SUBWAY IS OPENED IN BOSTON.

1900 L. FRANK BAUM PUBLISHES *THE WONDERFUL WIZARD OF OZ.*

26
THEODORE ROOSEVELT
(1858–1919)
President (1901–09)

The youngest man to become president, "TR" brought zest and vitality to the nation at the start of a new century. Though a sickly boy, he was a believer in the strenuous life and enjoyed boxing, judo, horseback riding, hiking, mountain climbing, and big-game hunting. The teddy bear was named for him.

BIOGRAPHY
Date of birth: October 27, 1858
Place of birth: New York City
Father: Theodore Roosevelt Sr. (1831–78)
Mother: Martha Bulloch Roosevelt (1834–84)
Wife: (1) Alice Hathaway Lee (1861–84); (2) Edith Kermit Carow (1861–1948)
Children: (1) 1; (2) 5
Date of death: January 6, 1919
Place of death: Oyster Bay, New York
Burial: Oyster Bay, New York
Terms: 2 (partial first term)
Dates of inaugurations: September 14, 1901; March 4, 1905
Age at first inauguration: 42
Vice president: Charles W. Fairbanks
Secretary of state: John Hay, Elihu Root, Robert Bacon
Secretary of treasury: Lyman J. Gage, Leslie M. Shaw, George B. Cortelyou

HIGHLIGHTS
1880 Graduated from Harvard College
October 27, 1880 Married Alice Hathaway Lee
1882–84 New York state assemblyman
1886 Candidate for mayor of New York City
December 2, 1886 Married Edith Kermit Carow
1889–95 Commissioner of U.S. Civil Service
1895–97 President of New York City police board
1897–98 Assistant secretary of the navy
1898 Colonel of the "Rough Riders" in Spanish–American War, leading charge on San Juan Hill
1899–1900 Governor of New York
1901 Vice president of the United States
1901–09 President of the United States
1903 Negotiated treaty with Panama giving United States rights to the "use, occupation, and control of" Canal Zone
1903 Established first federal bird reservation at Pelican Island, Florida
1904–05 Russo–Japanese War
1906 Awarded Nobel Peace Prize, the first American to win the award
1912 Defeated in presidential election

Puck cartoon, 1906, "King Teddy" Roosevelt with his chosen successor, Prince William Taft, on his shoulder.

"The president is merely the most important among a large number of public servants. He should be supported or opposed exactly to the degree which is warranted by his good conduct or bad conduct, his efficiency or inefficiency in rendering loyal, able, and disinterested service to the nation as a whole."

THEODORE ROOSEVELT

27
WILLIAM HOWARD TAFT
(1857–1930)
President (1909–13)

Taft is the only man to serve as president and also as a chief justice of the United States—his lifelong ambition.

BIOGRAPHY
Date of birth: September 15, 1857
Place of birth: Cincinnati, Ohio
Father: Alphonso Taft (1810–91)
Mother: Louisa Maria Torrey Taft (1827–1907)
Wife: Helen Herron (1861–1943)
Children: 3
Date of death: March 8, 1930
Place of death: Washington, D.C.
Burial: Arlington National Cemetery, Virginia
Terms: 1
Date of inauguration: March 4, 1909
Age at inauguration: 51
Vice president: James Schoolcraft Sherman
Secretary of state: Philander C. Knox
Secretary of treasury: Franklin MacVeagh

HIGHLIGHTS
1878 Graduated second in class of 132 students at Yale University
May 1880 Admitted to the bar before graduating from law school
1881–82 Assistant prosecutor of Hamilton County
1886 Married Helen Herron
1887–90 Judge of Cincinnati Superior Court
1904–08 Secretary of war
1908 Elected president
1912 New Mexico and Arizona admitted to the Union
1912 Nominated for election but defeated
1921 Appointed chief justice of the United States by President Warren Harding

1901

1913

1900 EASTMAN KODAK INTRODUCES THE BROWNIE BOX CAMERA.
1901 KING C. GILLETTE INVENTS THE FIRST SAFETY RAZOR WITH A DISPOSABLE BLADE.
1903 THE WRIGHT BROTHERS MAKE THE WORLD'S FIRST FLIGHT IN A HEAVIER-THAN-AIR MACHINE AT KITTY HAWK, NORTH CAROLINA.

1905 ALBERT EINSTEIN PRESENTS HIS THEORY OF SPECIAL RELATIVITY.
1908 FORD MOTOR COMPANY INTRODUCES THE MODEL T, PRICED AT $850.
1909 ADMIRAL ROBERT E. PEARY CLAIMS TO BE THE FIRST TO REACH THE NORTH POLE.

Joseph Pulitzer

1909 DR. SIGMUND FREUD BEGINS A LECTURE TOUR IN THE UNITED STATES.
1910 BOY SCOUTS OF AMERICA IS FOUNDED.
1910–20 THE MEXICAN REVOLUTION OCCURS.
1911 JOSEPH PULITZER CREATES PRIZES IN THE FIELDS OF FICTION, POETRY, HISTORY, AND JOURNALISM.
1912 AMERICAN GIRL GUIDES, NOW KNOWN AS AMERICAN SCOUTS, IS FOUNDED.

28
WOODROW WILSON
(1856–1924)
President (1913–21)

Highly educated, idealistic, and an inspiring speaker, Wilson led America's effort in World War I, saying, "The world must be made safe for democracy." His major defeat was the Senate's rejection of the League of Nations in 1919.

BIOGRAPHY
Date of birth: December 28, 1856
Place of birth: Staunton, Virginia
Father: Joseph Ruggles Wilson (1822–1903)
Mother: Janet Woodrow Wilson (1830–88)
Wife: (1) Ellen Louise Axson (1860–1914); (2) Edith Bolling Galt (1872–1961)
Children: (1) 3
Date of death: February 3, 1924
Place of death: Washington, D.C.
Burial: Washington, D.C.
Terms: 2
Dates of inaugurations: March 4, 1913; March 5, 1917
Age at first inauguration: 56
Vice president: Thomas R. Marshall
Secretary of state: William Jennings Bryan, Robert Lansing, Bainbridge Colby
Secretary of treasury: William G. McAdoo, Carter Glass, David F. Houston

HIGHLIGHTS
1879 Graduated from the College of New Jersey (now Princeton University)
1879–81 Attended University of Virginia law school
1882–83 Practiced law in Atlanta, Georgia
June 24, 1885 Married Ellen Louise Axson
1885–1902 Professor at Bryn Mawr College, Wesleyan University, and Princeton University; lectured at Johns Hopkins University
1886 Received Ph.D. in political science, Johns Hopkins University
1902–10 President of Princeton University
1911–13 Governor of New Jersey
1913–21 President of the United States

1913 Seventeenth Amendment ratified: election of senators by popular vote
December 18, 1915 Married Edith Bolling Galt
April 6, 1917 Declared war against Germany
1918 Issued Fourteen Points, the terms of peace; Germany signed armistice on November 11
1918 Awarded Nobel Peace Prize
1919 Eighteenth Amendment ratified: prohibition of alcoholic beverages
1920 Nineteenth Amendment ratified: women's right to vote

"It is not men that interest or disturb me primarily; it is ideas. Ideas live; men die."

WOODROW WILSON

Woodrow and Edith Wilson

"Liberty has never come from government. Liberty has always come from the subjects of it. The history of liberty is a history of limitations of governmental power, not the increase of it."

WOODROW WILSON

29
WARREN GAMALIEL HARDING
(1865–1923)
President (1921–23)

By 1923, as America's postwar depression was giving way to prosperity, Harding had wide popular support. Behind the scenes, crime and corruption marked his administration. Harding died before the scandals were revealed.

BIOGRAPHY
Date of birth: November 2, 1865
Place of birth: Blooming Grove, Ohio
Father: George Tryon Harding (1843–1928)
Mother: Phoebe Elizabeth Dickerson Harding (1843–1910)
Wife: Florence Kling De Wolfe (1860–1924)
Children: 1
Date of death: August 2, 1923
Place of death: San Francisco, California
Burial: Marion, Ohio
Terms: 1 (incomplete)
Date of inauguration: March 4, 1921
Age at inauguration: 55
Vice president: Calvin Coolidge
Secretary of state: Charles Evans Hughes
Secretary of treasury: Andrew W. Mellon

HIGHLIGHTS
1882 Graduated from Ohio Central College and taught school for one term
1884 With two partners, purchased the *Marion Star*
1891 Married Florence Mabel Kling De Wolfe, a divorcée with one son
1899–1903 Ohio state senator
1903–05 Lieutenant governor of Ohio
1915–21 U.S. senator
1920 Elected president
1921–23 Sale of nation's oil reserves led to the Teapot Dome Scandal—the most notorious of several scandals associated with the Harding presidency.
1921 Refused to support American membership in League of Nations

---

1913

1921

1921

1913 STAINLESS STEEL IS FIRST MANUFACTURED IN ENGLAND.
1914 THE ASSASSINATION OF AUSTRO-HUNGARIAN ARCHDUKE FRANZ FERDINAND TRIGGERS WORLD WAR I.
1917 AMERICA DECLARES WAR ON GERMANY AND SENDS TROOPS TO FRANCE.
1917 THE RUSSIAN REVOLUTION OCCURS.

Lenin

1918 INFLUENZA EPIDEMIC KILLS UP TO 50 MILLION PEOPLE WORLDWIDE.
1918 ARMISTICE ON NOVEMBER 11 ENDS WORLD WAR I.
1921 INSULIN, NECESSARY TO CONTROL DIABETES, IS FIRST ISOLATED BY DR. FREDERICK BANTING IN TORONTO, CANADA.

1922 TOMB OF TUTANKHAMEN IS DISCOVERED BY BRITISH ARCHAEOLOGIST HOWARD CARTER.
1922 *READER'S DIGEST* IS FOUNDED.
1922 THE FIRST SUCCESSFUL INSULIN TREATMENT OF DIABETES IS MADE.
1922 CONSTRUCTION BEGINS ON YANKEE STADIUM IN NEW YORK.

1921 At Birmingham, Alabama, accepted honorary degree from University of Alabama and lectured audience on racial equality

August 2, 1923 In San Francisco on cross-country "Voyage of Understanding," died at Palace Hotel, apparently of a stroke

"My God, this is a hell of a job! I have no trouble with my enemies. I can take care of my enemies in a fight. But my friends, my damn friends, they're the ones that keep me walking the floor nights."

WARREN G. HARDING

The Teapot Dome Scandal enmeshed some members of Harding's administration.

"I don't know what to do or where to turn in this taxation matter. Somewhere there must be a book that tells all about it, where I could go to straighten it out in my mind. But I don't know where the book is, and maybe I couldn't read it if I found it."

WARREN G. HARDING

೫ 30 ೫
CALVIN COOLIDGE
(1872–1929)
President (1923–29)

"Silent Cal," a man of few—but witty—words, was the beneficiary of the country's growth and prosperity. By the time the Great Depression hit in October 1929, Coolidge was in retirement.

BIOGRAPHY
Date of birth: July 4, 1872
Place of birth: Plymouth Notch, Vermont
Father: John Calvin Coolidge (1845–1926)
Mother: Victoria Josephine Moor Coolidge (1846–85)
Wife: Grace Anna Goodhue (1879–1957)
Children: 2
Date of death: January 5, 1933
Place of death: Northampton, Massachusetts
Burial: Plymouth, Vermont
Terms: 2 (partial first term)
Dates of inaugurations: August 3, 1923; March 4, 1925
Age at first inauguration: 51
Vice president: Charles G. Dawes
Secretary of state: Charles Evans Hughes, Frank B. Kellogg
Secretary of treasury: Andrew W. Mellon

HIGHLIGHTS
1897 Admitted to the bar
1919–20 Governor of Massachusetts
1921 Elected vice president
August 3, 1923 Sworn in as president at 2:47 a.m.
1924 Elected president
1924 Immigration Act cut immigration quota
1924 and 1926 Revenue acts reduced income and inheritance taxes, and abolished the gift tax and most excise taxes imposed during World War I
1927–28 Vetoed McNary-Haugen Bill for farm price supports

೫ 31 ೫
HERBERT C. HOOVER
(1874–1964)
President (1929–33)

Hoover brought a solid record of honesty and humanitarianism to his election. The stock market crash, just seven months after he took office, spiraled the nation into the Great Depression. Hoover became a scapegoat and was badly defeated in 1932.

BIOGRAPHY
Date of birth: August 10, 1874
Place of birth: West Branch, Iowa
Father: Jesse Clark Hoover (1846–80)
Mother: Huldah Minthorn Hoover (1848–83)
Wife: Lou Henry (1874–1944)
Children: 2
Date of death: October 20, 1964
Place of death: New York City
Burial: West Branch, Iowa
Terms: 1
Date of inauguration: March 4, 1929
Age at inauguration: 54
Vice president: Charles Curtis
Secretary of state: Henry L. Stimson
Secretary of treasury: Andrew W. Mellon, Ogden L. Mills

HIGHLIGHTS
1900 Helped defend foreign community in Tientsin during Boxer Rebellion
1908 Formed own engineering firm
1914 Headed American Relief Committee assisting Americans stranded in Europe
1917–18 As U.S. food administrator, urged meatless, wheatless days, to conserve supplies for war effort
1928 Elected president
1929 Agricultural Marketing Act created Federal Farm Board
October 29, 1929 Stock losses totaled billions of dollars as Dow Jones average, having peaked at 381, dropped, finally bottoming at 41 in 1932
1933 Twentieth Amendment ratified, moving presidential inauguration to January 20

1923

1933

1923 *TIME* MAGAZINE IS LAUNCHED.

1923 U.S. STEEL ADOPTS AN EIGHT-HOUR WORKDAY.

1923 THE KU KLUX KLAN DEFIES A LAW TO PUBLISH THE NAMES OF ITS MEMBERS.

1923 VLADIMIR ZWORYKIN FILES THE FIRST PATENT FOR COLOR TELEVISION.

1924 CLARENCE BIRDSEYE DEVELOPS AND MARKETS FIRST FROZEN FOOD.

1927 CHARLES LINDBERGH COMPLETES FIRST SOLO TRANSATLANTIC FLIGHT IN SINGLE-ENGINE PLANE, THE *SPIRIT OF ST. LOUIS*.

1929 A PROHIBITION-ERA CONFLICT BETWEEN TWO POWERFUL CRIMINAL GANGS LEADS TO THE MURDER OF SEVEN PEOPLE IN CHICAGO—AN EVENT KNOWN AS THE SAINT VALENTINE'S DAY MASSACRE.

1929 THE STOCK MARKET CRASHES, BEGINNING THE GREAT DEPRESSION.

1930 THE FIRST SUPERMARKET, KING KULLEN, OPENS IN NEW YORK CITY.

1931 THE EMPIRE STATE BUILDING OPENS IN NEW YORK CITY.

❦ 32 ❦
FRANKLIN DELANO ROOSEVELT
(1882–1945)
President (1933–45)

Charismatic and supremely confident, "FDR" was elected president a record four times. He rallied the nation through economic recovery with the New Deal and—with the Allies—led the strategy that brought victory during World War II.

BIOGRAPHY
Date of birth: January 30, 1882
Place of birth: Hyde Park, New York
Father: James Roosevelt (1828–1900)
Mother: Sara Delano Roosevelt (1854–1941)
Wife: Eleanor Roosevelt (1884–1962)
Children: 5
Date of death: April 12, 1945
Place of death: Warm Springs, Georgia
Burial: Hyde Park, New York
Terms: 4 (incomplete fourth term)
Dates of inaugurations: March 4, 1933; January 20, 1937; January 20, 1941; January 20, 1945
Age at first inauguration: 51
Vice president: John Nance Garner, Henry A. Wallace, Harry S. Truman
Secretary of state: Cordell Hull, Edward R. Stettinius Jr.
Secretary of treasury: W. H. Woodin, Henry Morgenthau Jr.

HIGHLIGHTS
1903 Received degree from Harvard University
1904–07 Attended Columbia University Law School
March 17, 1905 Married Eleanor Roosevelt
1907 Admitted to the bar
1911–13 New York state senator
1913–20 Assistant secretary of the navy
1919 Crippled by an attack of polio
1920 Ran unsuccessfully as Democratic nominee for vice president
1921 Returned to private life as lawyer and politician

1929–32 Governor of New York
1932 Elected president of the United States
1933–35 Launched New Deal programs, including National Industrial Recovery Act (NIRA) and Works Progress Administration (WPA)
1933 Repealed Eighteenth amendment (Prohibition)
1935 Social Security legislation passed
1937 Proposed to appoint a new Supreme Court justice, up to maximum of six, for each sitting justice seventy or older with at least ten years of service; its Senate sponsor died and the bill was never brought to a vote
December 7, 1941 Japan attacks Pearl Harbor
1941–45 Led U.S. home front and armed forces through World War II
1941 Met with British Prime Minister Winston Churchill, and drafted Atlantic Charter, which ultimately provided the basis for the United Nations Charter
1942 Amid hysterical fear of possible Japanese attack on mainland, signed Executive Order 9066 requiring internment of 120,000 persons of Japanese descent living in the United States
1945 Attended Yalta Conference with Churchill and Chairman Josef Stalin to discuss Soviet participation in Pacific war and postwar settlement

"Today, in this year of war, 1945, we have learned lessons—at fearful cost—and we shall profit by them. We have learned that we cannot live alone, at peace; that our own well-being is dependent on the well-being of other nations far away. We have learned that we must live as men, not as ostriches, nor as dogs in the manger. We have learned to be citizens of the world, members of the human community. We have learned the simple truth, as Emerson said, that 'The only way to have a friend is to be one.'"

FRANKLIN D. ROOSEVELT, FOURTH INAUGURAL ADDRESS, JANUARY 20, 1945

❦ 33 ❦
HARRY S. TRUMAN
(1884–1972)
President (1945–53)

Honest, decisive, stubborn, and blunt in speech, Truman thrived on the political life and was an avid student of history. The first president to take office in wartime; he authorized the atomic bombing of Hiroshima and Nagasaki. Guiding the nation to a peacetime economy, he launched a domestic program, the Fair Deal. In 1948 he approved a major foreign-aid program for European recovery.

BIOGRAPHY
Date of birth: May 8, 1884
Place of birth: Lamar, Missouri
Father: John Anderson Truman (1851–1914)
Mother: Martha Ellen Young Truman (1852–1947)
Wife: Elizabeth "Bess" Wallace (1885–1982)
Children: 1
Date of death: December 26, 1972
Place of death: Kansas City, Missouri
Burial: Independence, Missouri
Terms: 2 (incomplete first term)
Dates of inaugurations: April 12, 1945; January 20, 1949
Age at first inauguration: 60
Vice president: Alben W. Barkley
Secretary of state: Edward R. Stettinius Jr., James F. Byrnes, George C. Marshall, Dean G. Acheson
Secretary of treasury: Henry Morgenthau Jr., Frederick M. Vinson, John W. Snyder

HIGHLIGHTS
1901 Graduated from Independence High School in Missouri
1905 Enlisted in the National Guard and served in it until 1911
1905 Passed an eye exam by memorizing the eye chart, although his eyesight had been 20/50 in his right eye and 20/400 in his left
1917–19 Served with an artillery battery in World War I, rising to rank of major
June 28, 1919 Married Elizabeth "Bess" Wallace

1936 MACMILLAN PUBLISHES MARGARET MITCHELL'S *GONE WITH THE WIND*.

1937 THE *HINDENBURG* DISASTER TAKES PLACE.

1937 WALT DISNEY RELEASES THE FIRST FULL-LENGTH ANIMATED FEATURE: *SNOW WHITE AND THE SEVEN DWARFS*.

1939 THE WORLD'S FAIR OPENS IN NEW YORK.

1939 WORLD WAR II BEGINS.

1944 ON JUNE 6, "D-DAY," THE ALLIED TROOPS LAND AT NORMANDY, BEGINNING THE MARCH ACROSS EUROPE TO DEFEAT HITLER.

1945 GERMANY SURRENDERS MAY 10 AND JAPAN SURRENDERS SEPTEMBER 2.

1945 GRAND RAPIDS, MICHIGAN, BEGINS THE FIRST FLUORIDATION OF WATER, TO REDUCE TOOTH DECAY.

1945 JACKIE ROBINSON JOINS THE BROOKLYN DODGERS, BREAKING THE COLOR BARRIER IN MAJOR LEAGUE BASEBALL.

1946 DR. SPOCK'S *BABY AND CHILD CARE* IS PUBLISHED AS BABY BOOM BEGINS.

1947 TEST PILOT CHUCK YEAGER BECOMES THE FIRST TO BREAK THE SOUND BARRIER.

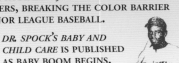

Jackie Robinson

1919–22 Established a haberdashery in Kansas City, Missouri

1926–34 County judge and presiding judge of Jackson County, Missouri

1935–45 U.S. senator from Missouri

March–April 1945 Vice president of the United States

April 12, 1945 President of the United States at Roosevelt's death

August 6 and 9, 1945 Ordered the atomic bomb to be dropped on Hiroshima and Nagasaki, Japan

January 10, 1946 First meeting of UN General Assembly in London

1948 Reelected president in famous upset victory over Republican Thomas E. Dewey

1948 Approved the Marshall Plan to rebuild Europe

1949 Helped establish the North Atlantic Treaty Organization (NATO)

1950–53 Korean War; Truman relieved General Douglas MacArthur of his command in April 1951

1951 Twenty-second Amendment ratified, limiting future presidents to two terms in office

"If you can't stand the heat, stay out of the kitchen."

HARRY S. TRUMAN

The Chicago Daily Tribune jumped the gun in declaring the outcome of the 1948 presidential election.

"You, more than any other man, have saved Western civilization."

WINSTON CHURCHILL TO HARRY S. TRUMAN

◦ 34 ◦
DWIGHT D. EISENHOWER
(1890–1969)
President (1953–61)

The famous Eisenhower smile reflected the friendly, gregarious man who inspired America's confidence and respect. A career soldier, hero-worshipped after World War II, he was elected twice with huge majorities, and led the nation at the onset of the space age and the escalation of the cold war between Communist countries and Western democracies.

BIOGRAPHY

Date of birth: October 14, 1890
Place of birth: Denison, Texas
Father: David Jacob Eisenhower (1863–1942)
Mother: Ida Elizabeth Stover Eisenhower (1862–1946)
Wife: Mamie Geneva Doud (1896–1979)
Children: 2
Date of death: March 28, 1969
Place of death: Washington, D.C.
Burial: Abilene, Kansas
Terms: 2
Dates of inaugurations: January 20, 1953; January 21, 1957
Age at first inauguration: 62
Vice president: Richard M. Nixon
Secretary of state: John Foster Dulles, Christian A. Herter
Secretary of treasury: George M. Humphrey, Robert B. Anderson

HIGHLIGHTS

1911–15 Attended West Point
July 1, 1916 Married Mamie Geneva Doud
1917–18 Commander of Tank Corps Training Center in Camp Colt, Pennsylvania
1932–35 Aide to General Douglas MacArthur, chief of staff of the U.S. Army

1935–39 Senior military assistant to General Douglas MacArthur in the Philippine Islands

1942 Appointed commanding general of U.S. forces in Europe

1943–45 Supreme commander of Allied Expeditionary Force in Europe

1948–50 President of Columbia University

1951–52 Appointed supreme commander of NATO

1952 Vice President Nixon defended acceptance of gift of a dog for his daughters in speech responding to allegations of political slush fund

1952 Elected president of the United States

July 1953 Korean War armistice signed

1954 Landmark Supreme Court desegregation decision *Brown v. Board of Education*

1954 Senator Joseph McCarthy's hunt for Communists in government culminates in televised Army-McCarthy hearings, which exposed lack of solid evidence; soon thereafter the Senate voted to censure him

1956 State of president's health following heart attack became a campaign issue

1956 Reelected to a second term as president

1957 Dispatched federal troops to Little Rock, Arkansas, high school to protect black students

1957 Succeeded in forming International Atomic Energy Agency, a plan for peaceful use of nuclear energy

October 1957 Russia launched Sputnik, first manmade space satellite

1959 Russian Premier Krushchev visited the United States

1959 Broke off diplomatic relations with China

1959 Hawaii and Alaska admitted to the Union

1960 Russia shot down American U-2 plane

"The United States never lost a soldier or a foot of ground in my administration. We kept the peace. People ask how it happened—by God, it didn't just happen, I'll tell you that."

DWIGHT D. EISENHOWER

1953   1961

1948 ISRAEL BECOMES A STATE.

1948 THE TRANSISTOR IS INTRODUCED.

1948 PEOPLE'S REPUBLIC OF CHINA IS ESTABLISHED.

1949 *PEANUTS* COMIC STRIP BY CHARLES SCHULZ APPEARS.

1950 DINERS CLUB, THE FIRST MODERN CREDIT CARD, IS INTRODUCED.

1951 LITTLE, BROWN PUBLISHES J.D. SALINGER'S *THE CATCHER IN THE RYE.*

1951 *I LOVE LUCY* WITH LUCILLE BALL AND DESI ARNAZ PREMIERES ON TELEVISION.

1952 SALK TESTS POLIO VACCINE.

1953 DOUBLE HELIX STRUCTURE OF DNA IS DISCOVERED.

Lucille Ball

1953 C.A. SWANSON & SONS INTRODUCES THE FIRST TV DINNER.

1955 ROSA PARKS REFUSES TO GIVE HER SEAT ON A BUS TO A WHITE MAN, IN MONTGOMERY, ALABAMA.

1955 ELVIS PRESLEY'S APPEARANCE ON *THE ED SULLIVAN SHOW* SETS A RECORD OF VIEWERS.

1959 FIRST DOMESTIC JET AIRLINE PASSENGER SERVICE IN U.S. BEGINS.

1959 BARBIE DOLL AND PANTY HOSE ARE INTRODUCED.

✦ 35 ✦
JOHN F. KENNEDY
(1917–63)
President (1961–63)

"An idealist without illusions" was how Kennedy described himself. The youngest man, and the first Roman Catholic, to be elected president, Kennedy captured the imagination of America's youth with his New Frontier program. He was assassinated after two years, ten months in office.

BIOGRAPHY

Date of birth: May 29, 1917
Place of birth: Brookline, Massachusetts
Father: Joseph Patrick Kennedy (1888–1969)
Mother: Rose Fitzgerald Kennedy (1890–1995)
Wife: Jacqueline Lee Bouvier (1929–94)
Children: 3
Date of death: November 22, 1963
Place of death: Dallas, Texas
Burial: Arlington National Cemetery, Virginia
Terms: 1 (incomplete)
Date of inauguration: January 20, 1961
Age at inauguration: 43
Vice president: Lyndon B. Johnson
Secretary of state: Dean Rusk
Secretary of treasury: C. Douglas Dillon

HIGHLIGHTS

1935 Attended Princeton University
1940 Graduated from Harvard University
1940–41 Attended Stanford University Business School
1941–45 Served in the U.S. Navy and earned a Purple Heart; when his PT boat was sunk, his bravery enabled his crew to survive
1947–53 U.S. representative from Massachusetts
1953–61 U.S. senator from Massachusetts
September 12, 1953 Married Jacqueline Lee Bouvier

1957 Won the Pulitzer Prize for his book *Profiles in Courage*
1961–63 President of the United States
1961–63 Continued sending advisers and military supplies, started under Eisenhower, to South Vietnam
1961 Established the Peace Corps, a volunteer agency to support underdeveloped countries
1961 Unsuccessful Bay of Pigs invasion, an American-led attempt to overthrow Fidel Castro
1961 Kennedy stated objective to put a man on the moon by end of decade
1961 Twenty-third Amendment ratified, giving residents of District of Columbia the right to vote in presidential elections
October 1962 Cuban Missile Crisis; Russia dismantled missile bases in Cuba
1962–63 Promoted legislative programs to end desegregation in education, housing, and employment
1963 Nuclear Test Ban Treaty with Britain and Soviet Union, later signed by more than 100 countries
November 22, 1963 Assassinated in Dallas, Texas

"In the long history of the world, only a few generations have been granted the role of defending freedom in this hour of maximum danger. I do not shrink from this responsibility—I welcome it. I do not believe that any of us would exchange places with any other people or any other generation. The energy, the faith, the devotion which we bring to this endeavor will light our country and all who serve it—and the glow from that fire can truly light the world. And so, my fellow Americans: ask not what your country can do for you—ask what you can do for your country."

JOHN F. KENNEDY, FROM HIS INAUGURAL ADDRESS, JANUARY 20, 1961

✦ 36 ✦
LYNDON B. JOHNSON
(1908–73)
President (1963–69)

Johnson was a complex personality, a man who relished power and a master manipulator in Congress. He had a major success in his extensive domestic program "The Great Society," and a major defeat for his policy of escalating the Vietnam War.

BIOGRAPHY

Date of birth: August 27, 1908
Place of birth: Stonewall, Texas
Father: Sam Ealy Johnson Jr. (1877–1937)
Mother: Rebekah Baines (1881–1958)
Wife: Claudia "Lady Bird" Taylor (1912–2007)
Children: 2
Date of death: January 22, 1973
Place of death: Johnson City, Texas
Burial: Stonewall, Texas
Terms: 2 (partial first term)
Dates of inaugurations: November 22, 1963; January 20, 1965
Age at first inauguration: 55
Vice president: Hubert Humphrey
Secretary of state: Dean Rusk
Secretary of treasury: C. Douglas Dillon, Henry H. Fowler, Joseph W. Barr

HIGHLIGHTS

1927–30 Attended Southwest Texas State Teachers College
1930–31 Taught public speaking and debate at Sam Houston High School in Houston, Texas
1931–35 Secretary to U.S. representative Richard M. Kleberg
November 17, 1934 Married Claudia "Lady Bird" Taylor
1935–37 Director of the National Youth Administration in Texas
1937–48 U.S. representative from Texas
1940–42 Served in World War II as lieutenant commander in U.S. Navy; awarded the Silver Star

1961

1963

1963

1961 COSMONAUT YURI GAGARIN BECOMES THE FIRST HUMAN IN SPACE. THREE WEEKS LATER, ALAN SHEPARD, ABOARD MERCURY CAPSULE *FREEDOM 7*, IS THE FIRST AMERICAN IN SPACE.

1962 THE CUBAN MISSILE CRISIS OCCURS.

1962 MARILYN MONROE DIES.

1962 JOHN GLENN JR. BECOMES THE FIRST AMERICAN IN ORBIT WHEN HE CIRCLES THE EARTH THREE TIMES.

1962 JAMES MEREDITH BECOMES THE FIRST BLACK STUDENT AT THE UNIVERSITY OF MISSISSIPPI AFTER TROOPS PUT DOWN RIOTS.

1963 MARTIN LUTHER KING JR. DELIVERS HIS "I HAVE A DREAM" SPEECH AT THE MARCH ON WASHINGTON.

John Glenn Jr.

1964 TONKIN GULF RESOLUTION ESCALATES AMERICAN INVOLVEMENT IN VIETNAM.
1964 CIVIL RIGHTS ACT IS PASSED.
1964 BEATLEMANIA SEIZES AMERICA WHEN THE FAB FOUR VISIT.
1965 MALCOLM X IS ASSASSINATED AT THE AUDUBON BALLROOM IN HARLEM, NEW YORK.
1965 RACE RIOTS OCCUR OVER SIX DAYS IN THE WATTS NEIGHBORHOOD OF LOS ANGELES.

1948–60 U.S. senator from Texas

1961–63 Vice president of the United States

1963–69 President of the United States

1964 Civil Rights Act passed, barring discrimination in employment, protecting the right to vote, and guaranteeing access to public accommodations, among other things

1964 Twenty-fourth Amendment ratified, outlawing poll tax

1964–68 Escalated U.S. role in Vietnam, building troop level to over half a million

1965 Medicare and Medicaid programs established

1965–67 Four environmental protection acts passed to improve air and water quality

1967 Twenty-fifth Amendment ratified, allowing presidents to fill a vacancy in vice presidency

Lyndon Johnson's charisma was reflected in his Great Society legislation—the most ambitious in U.S. history.

"He can be as gentle and solicitous as a nurse, but as ruthless and deceptive as a riverboat gambler."

ROWLAND EVANS AND ROBERT NOVAK
ON LYNDON B. JOHNSON

◈ 37 ◈
RICHARD MILHOUS NIXON
(1913–94)
President (1969–74)

Lonely, hypersensitive, dishonest, intelligent, decisive, courageous. Words describing Nixon are as conflicted as his record. In his first term he greatly improved relations with Russia and China, and ended U.S. involvement in Vietnam. His second term was destroyed by the Watergate scandal that forced him to resign.

BIOGRAPHY

Date of birth: January 9, 1913
Place of birth: Yorba Linda, California
Father: Francis Anthony Nixon (1878–1956)
Mother: Hannah Milhous Nixon (1885–1967)
Wife: Thelma Catherine "Pat" Ryan (1912–93)
Children: 2
Date of death: April 22, 1994
Place of death: New York City
Burial: Yorba Linda, California
Terms: 2 (partial second term)
Dates of inaugurations: January 20, 1969; January 20, 1973
Age at first inauguration: 56
Vice president: Spiro Agnew, Gerald R. Ford
Secretary of state: William P. Rogers, Henry A. Kissinger
Secretary of treasury: David M. Kennedy, John B. Connally Jr., George P. Shultz, William E. Simon

HIGHLIGHTS

1934 Graduated from Whittier College

1937 Received degree from Duke University Law School in Durham, North Carolina

1937–41 Practiced law in Whittier, California

1938 Was cast in the Whittier Community Players production of *The Dark Tower*, where he played opposite of a school teacher named Thelma "Pat" Ryan

June 21, 1940 Married Thelma Catherine "Pat" Ryan

1942–46 Worked briefly in the Office of Price Administration in Washington, D.C.

1947–50 U.S. representative from California

1948 Supported the Taft-Hartley Act

1951–53 U.S. senator from California

1953–61 Vice president of the United States

1960 Republican nominee for president, defeated by Kennedy

1962 Defeated in election for governor of California

1963–68 Practiced law in New York City

1969–74 President of the United States

1969–74 Vietnam War: Despite 1973 peace agreement ending U.S. involvement, fighting continued between North and South Vietnam

July 20, 1969 Astronaut Neil Armstrong, commander of Apollo 11, sets foot on the moon

April 30, 1970 Announced the incursion of U.S. troops into Cambodia to disrupt so-called North Vietnamese sanctuaries

1971 Twenty-sixth amendment ratified, lowering the voting age to eighteen

1972 Nixon was first president to visit China, opening relations with the communist government

1972 Strategic Arms Limitation Talks (SALT) agreement signed with Soviet leader Brezhnev

June 17, 1972 Five agents from the Committee to Reelect the President arrested after burglarizing Democratic National Committee offices at the Watergate office complex

August 9, 1974 Resigned to avoid impeachment

April 18, 1994 Suffered a stroke and died four days later at the age of eighty-one

"No words can describe the depths of my regret and pain at the anguish my mistakes over Watergate have caused the nation and the presidency, a nation I so deeply love and an institution I so greatly respect."

RICHARD M. NIXON, SEPTEMBER 1974

1965

1974

1965 THE MEDICARE BILL IS SIGNED, PROVIDING HEALTH INSURANCE FOR AMERICANS OVER SIXTY-FIVE.

1967 THE FIRST ISSUE OF *ROLLING STONE* MAGAZINE IS ISSUED.

1967 APOLLO 8 ORBITS THE MOON DURING A FIVE-DAY MISSION.

Martin Luther King Jr.

1968 JAMES EARL RAY ASSASSINATES MARTIN LUTHER KING JR. AT THE LORRAINE MOTEL IN MEMPHIS.

1968 ROBERT F. KENNEDY IS KILLED BY SIRHAN SIRHAN IN LOS ANGELES.

1969 *SESAME STREET* AIRS ON PUBLIC TV FOR THE FIRST TIME.

1969 WOODSTOCK FESTIVAL OPENS IN UPSTATE NEW YORK.

1970 THE NATIONAL GUARD KILLS FOUR STUDENT ANTI-WAR PROTESTORS AT KENT STATE.

1970 THE WORLD TRADE CENTER IS BUILT.

❧ 38 ❧
GERALD RUDOLPH FORD
(1913–2006)
President (1974–77)

Ford was the first man appointed to the vice presidency under the new Twenty-fifth Amendment, replacing Spiro Agnew. Just a year later, he took the oath as president, at the climax of the Watergate scandal, upon Nixon's resignation.

BIOGRAPHY

Date of birth: July 14, 1913
Place of birth: Omaha, Nebraska
Father: Leslie Lynch King (1882–1941)
Adoptive father: Gerald Rudolf Ford (1890–1962)
Mother: Dorothy Ayer Gardner (1892–1967)
Wife: Elizabeth Bloomer Warren (1918–
Children: 4
Date of death: December 26, 2006
Place of death: Rancho Mirage, California
Burial: Grand Rapids, Michigan
Terms: 1 (partial)
Date of inauguration: August 9, 1974
Age at inauguration: 61
Vice president: Nelson A. Rockefeller
Secretary of state: Henry A. Kissinger
Secretary of treasury: William E. Simon

HIGHLIGHTS

1935 Graduated from the University of Michigan
1935–41 Boxing coach and assistant football coach
1941 Received degree from Yale Law School
1941 Admitted to the bar
1942–46 Served in the U.S. Navy, rising to lieutenant commander
October 15, 1948 Married Elizabeth "Betty" Bloomer Warren
1949–73 U.S. representative from Michigan
1973 Appointed vice president of the United States, at Spiro Agnew's resignation
1974–77 President of the United States after Nixon's resignation

September 1974 Granted pardon to Nixon
1974 Appointed Nelson Rockefeller vice president
1974 Offered conditional amnesty to Vietnam War draft evaders and deserters
1974 First American president to visit Japan
1974 Congress denied request for more aid to South Vietnam
1975 Signed legislation extending $2.3 billion in short-term loans to New York City, on the brink of default
1975 Approved seven-year extension of 1965 Voting Rights Act
1975 Signed Helsinki Agreement, guaranteeing the European boundaries established after World War II

"A government big enough to give you everything you want is a government big enough to take from you everything you have."

GERALD R. FORD

A young Gerald R. Ford, at a Kent County farm during his campaign for Congress

"I cannot imagine any other country in the world where the opposition would seek, and the chief executive would allow, the dissemination of his most private and personal conversations with his staff, which, to be honest, do not exactly confer sainthood on anyone concerned."

GERALD R. FORD

❧ 39 ❧
JIMMY CARTER
(1924–)
President (1977–81)

Born James Earl Carter Jr. (he took the oath of office as "Jimmy"), Carter—a Southern Democrat—vigorously supported the rights of blacks and women and all oppressed people throughout the world. His greatest triumph was the 1979 Middle east peace treaty, and his greatest defeat was the Iran hostage crisis.

BIOGRAPH

Date of birth: October 1, 1924
Place of birth: Plains, Georgia
Father: James Earl Carter Sr. (1894–1953)
Mother: Lillian Gordy (1898–1983)
Wife: Rosalynn Smith (1927–   )
Children: 4
Terms: 1
Date of inauguration: January 20, 1977
Age at inauguration: 52
Vice president: Walter F. Mondale
Secretary of state: Cyrus R. Vance, Edmund S. Muskie
Secretary of treasury: W. Michael Blumenthal, G. William Miller

HIGHLIGHTS

1946 Graduated from U.S. Military Academy at West Point
July 7, 1946 Married Rosalynn Smith
1946–53 Served in U.S. Navy, rising to rank of lieutenant
1963–67 Senator in Georgia legislature
1971–75 Governor of Georgia
1977–81 President of the United States
1977 Panama Canal Treaty, relinquishing Canal Zone to Panama
1978 Camp David accords, leading to Middle East peace treaty in 1979
1979 Established diplomatic relations with China
November 4, 1979 American hostages taken captive in Iran
1980 Defeated in bid for second term
1980–present Continues humanitarian work at Carter Center and Habitat for Humanity; author of memoirs, poetry, and fiction
2002 Awarded Nobel Peace Prize

1974

1977

1977

1975 *SATURDAY NIGHT LIVE* PREMIERES ON TELEVISION.

1975 JOHN N. MITCHELL, H. R. HALDEMAN, AND JOHN D. EHRLICHMAN ARE FOUND GUILTY OF WATERGATE COVER-UP; SENTENCED FROM THIRTY MONTHS TO EIGHT YEARS IN JAIL.

1976 THE UNITED STATES CELEBRATES THE **200**TH ANNIVERSARY OF THE DECLARATION OF INDEPENDENCE.

1977 APPLE COMPUTERS INTRODUCES THE FIRST COMMERCIAL PERSONAL COMPUTER.

1977 ELVIS PRESLEY DIES AT AGE FORTY-TWO.

1977 OPTICAL FIBER IS USED FOR THE FIRST TIME TO CARRY LIVE TELEPHONE TRAFFIC.

1977 FIRST *STAR WARS* FILM IS PRODUCED.

1979 FIRST "TEST-TUBE BABY" IS BORN.

1979 PARTIAL MELTDOWN AT THREE MILE ISLAND (PENNSYLVANIA) NUCLEAR GENERATING STATION RESULTS IN RELEASE OF SIGNIFICANT AMOUNT OF RADIOACTIVITY. NO DEATHS OR INJURIES RESULTED.

40
RONALD REAGAN
(1911–2004)
President (1981–89)

The oldest U.S. president on taking office, and the only president with "professional actor" on his résumé, Reagan was called the Great Communicator. Cheerful, even-tempered, always optimistic, he achieved most of his domestic economic goals and signed a historic arms reduction treaty with the Soviet Union.

BIOGRAPHY
Date of birth: February 6, 1911
Place of birth: Tampico, Illinois
Father: John Edward Reagan (1883–1941)
Mother: Nelle Wilson (1885–1962)
Wife: (1) Jane Wyman (1914–2007); (2) Nancy Davis (1921–   )
Children: (1) 2; (2) 2
Date of death: June 5, 2004
Place of death: Bel Air, California
Burial: Simi Valley, California
Terms: 2
Dates of inaugurations: January 20, 1981; January 21, 1985
Age at first inauguration: 69
Vice president: George H. W. Bush
Secretary of state: Alexander M. Haig Jr., George P. Shultz
Secretary of treasury: Donald T. Regan, James A. Baker III, Nicholas F. Brady

HIGHLIGHTS
1932–37 Graduated from Eureka College, Illinois
1934 Radio sports announcer in Des Moines, Iowa
1937 Hollywood screen test and first movie offer, *Love Is on the Air*
1937–65 Actor and president (seven times) of Screen Actors Guild
January 25, 1940 Married actress Jane Wyman; divorced in 1948
1942 Appeared in *Kings Row*; years later took title for his autobiography from one of his lines in the film, "Where's the rest of me?"
1942–45 Captain in U.S. Army Air Force
March 4, 1952 Married Nancy Davis
1952–62 Host of General Electric Theatre
1964 Television speech supporting Republican presidential nominee Barry Goldwater drew more contributions than any other political speech until then
1967–75 Governor of California
1981–89 President of the United States
March 30, 1981 Wounded in assassination attempt
1983 Signed into law a bill to ensure Social Security system's solvency beyond the year 2050
1982–87 "Reaganomics" produced longest economic expansion to date in peacetime since World War II, but saw deficits rise as well
1983–88 Terrorist attacks against U.S. and Western nations
1985–88 Series of summit meetings with Soviet leader Gorbachev on nuclear arms reduction
November 1986 The country learned that the government had sold weapons to Iran to obtain release of hostages; further, money from these sales had illegally gone to Nicaraguan Contras in support of their battle against the Sandinista government

"What I'd really like to do is go down in history as the president who made Americans believe in themselves again."

RONALD REAGAN, 1981

"My view is that President Gorbachev is different from previous Soviet leaders. . . . I want the new closeness to continue . . . as long as they continue to act in a helpful manner. If and when they don't, then first pull your punches. If they persist, pull the plug. It's still trust but verify; it's still play but cut the cards."

RONALD REAGAN, FAREWELL ADDRESS, 1989

41
GEORGE HERBERT WALKER BUSH
(1924–   )
President (1989–93)

Despite a sluggish economy and unfilled promises on the domestic front, Bush earned respect even from critics for his leadership in foreign policy. He signed major nuclear disarmament treaties, presided over the end of the cold war, and saw the collapse of Communism and the Soviet Union.

BIOGRAPHY
Date of birth: June 12, 1924
Place of birth: Milton, Massachusetts
Father: Prescott S. Bush (1895–1972)
Mother: Dorothy Walker (1901–92)
Wife: Barbara Pierce (1925–   )
Children: 6
Terms: 1
Date of inauguration: January 20, 1989
Age at inauguration: 64
Vice president: J. Danforth "Dan" Quayle
Secretary of state: James A. Baker III, Lawrence Eagleburger
Secretary of treasury: Nicholas F. Brady

HIGHLIGHTS
1942–45 Served in U.S. Navy in World War II, receiving Distinguished Flying Cross
January 6, 1945 Married Barbara Pierce
1948 Yale University
1948–66 Oil businessman in Texas; formed own company in 1953
1966 Elected U.S. representative from Texas
1971–74 U.S. ambassador to United Nations
1974–75 Chief, U.S. Liaison Office in Beijing, China
1976–77 Director, Central Intelligence Agency
1981–89 Vice president of the United States
1989–93 President of the United States
1989 Tiananmen Square demonstration in Beijing, China
1989–90 Invasion of Panama and capture of General Manuel Antonio Noriega
1989–92 End of the cold war and collapse of Communism in eastern Europe and Soviet Union

1981   1993

1980 JOHN LENNON IS SHOT AND KILLED BY MARK DAVID CHAPMAN IN NEW YORK CITY.
1981 SANDRA DAY O'CONNOR IS CONFIRMED AS FIRST WOMAN JUSTICE OF SUPREME COURT.
1983 SALLY RIDE BECOMES THE FIRST AMERICAN WOMAN TO TRAVEL IN SPACE.

1983 COMPACT DISCS ARE INTRODUCED BY SONY AND PHILIPS.
1986 SPACE SHUTTLE CHALLENGER EXPLODES SECONDS AFTER TAKEOFF.
1987 WALL STREET CRASHES AND THE DOW JONES INDUSTRIAL AVERAGE DROPS BY **508** POINTS ON OCTOBER 19.
1987 FIRST USE OF AZT IS APPROVED TO FIGHT AIDS.

1988 PAM AM FLIGHT **103** EXPLODES AND CRASHES IN LOCKERBIE, SCOTLAND.
1989 TANKER EXXON *VALDEZ* RUNS AGROUND OFF COAST OF ALASKA, CAUSING THE LARGEST OIL SPILL IN U.S. HISTORY.
1989 BERLIN WALL FALLS.

1992 REPRESENTATIVES FROM UP TO **180** COUNTRIES MEET IN RIO DE JANEIRO FOR THE UN EARTH SUMMIT.

1990–91 Persian Gulf War
1990–93 With Russian Presidents Gorbachev and Yeltsin, signed series of agreements on reduction of strategic arms
1992 Sent U.S. troops to aid Somalia

". . . a brilliant diversity spread like stars, like a thousand points of light in a broad and peaceful sky."

❧ 42 ❧
WILLIAM JEFFERSON CLINTON
(1946–)
President (1993–2001)

One of the brightest and most empathetic politicians, Clinton presided over the longest peacetime economic expansion in U.S. history. His unprecedented popular approval ratings survived his personal indiscretions and an impeachment trial.

BIOGRAPHY
Date of birth: August 19, 1946
Place of birth: Hope, Arkansas
Father: William Jefferson Blythe III (1917–46); took name of stepfather Roger Clinton
Mother: Virginia Cassidy Blythe (1923–94)
Wife: Hillary Rodham (1947–)
Children: 1
Terms: 2
Age at first inauguration: 46
Dates of inaugurations: January 20, 1993; January 20, 1997
Vice president: Al Gore
Secretary of state: Warren Christopher, Madeleine Albright
Secretary of treasury: Robert Rubin

HIGHLIGHTS
1968 Graduated from Georgetown University
1968–70 Attended Oxford University, England, as Rhodes Scholar
1973 Graduated from Yale Law School

1973–76 Taught at University of Arkansas at Fayetteville
October 11, 1975 Married Hillary Rodham
1976 Elected attorney general of Arkansas
1979–81 and 1983–92 Governor of Arkansas for five terms
1993–2001 President of the United States
1993 Whitewater affair investigations began
1993 Health care reform bill defeated
1994 North American Free Trade Agreement (NAFTA) and General Agreement on Tariffs and Trade (GATT) passed
1995 Oklahoma City federal building bombed
1995–96 Intervened in Bosnia conflict
1997 Balanced Budget Act
1998 Monica Lewinsky scandal; Clinton testified before federal grand jury
1998 Middle East agreement signed between Palestinians and Israel
December 19, 1998 Congress voted to impeach Clinton
February 12, 1999 Senate voted to acquit Clinton
1999 Kosovo bombed; peace treaty signed
1999 Financial Reform Bill signed
2000 Breakdown of talks between Palestinians and Israel at Camp David

"Our democracy must be not only the envy of the world but the engine of our own renewal. There is nothing wrong with America that cannot be cured by what is right with America."

WILLIAM J. CLINTON, FIRST INAUGURAL ADDRESS, JANUARY 20, 1993

"The new rage is to say that the government is the cause of all our problems, and if only we had no government, we'd have no problems. I can tell you, that contradicts evidence, history, and common sense."

WILLIAM J. CLINTON

❧ 43 ❧
GEORGE WALKER BUSH
(1946–)
President (2001–09)

After a tumultuous first term, George Bush won reelection in 2004, defeating John Kerry in one of the largest voter turnouts in American history. On September 11, 2001, just eight months into his first term—which he had won largely on a domestic platform—George Bush became a war president. Dedicating himself to defeating global terrorism, he attacked the Taliban in Afghanistan and invaded Iraq. The decision to invade Iraq became an important issue in the 2004 election.

BIOGRAPHY
Date of birth: July 6, 1946
Place of birth: New Haven, Connecticut
Father: George Herbert Walker Bush (1924–)
Mother: Barbara Pierce Bush (1925–)
Wife: Laura Welch (1946–)
Children: 2
Terms: 2
Age at first inauguration: 54
Dates of inaugurations: January 20, 2001; January 20, 2005
Vice president: Richard Cheney
Secretary of state: Colin Powell, Condoleezza Rice
Secretary of treasury: Paul H. O'Neill, John W. Snow, Henry M. Paulson Jr.

HIGHLIGHTS
1968 Graduated from Yale University
1968–73 Served in the Texas Air National Guard
1975 Graduated from Harvard Business School
November 5, 1977 Married Laura Welch
1978 Defeated in election to U.S. House of Representatives
1989–93 Managing partner, Texas Rangers baseball team
1995–2000 Governor of Texas
November 7, 2000 Election Day; no clear winner in presidential contest with Al Gore

---

1993

1993 A BOMB EXPLODES BENEATH THE WORLD TRADE CENTER, KILLING SIX PEOPLE, ON FEBRUARY 26.
1993 FBI OFFICERS STORM THE BRANCH DAVIDIAN COMPOUND AT WACO, TEXAS, AND SEVENTY-SIX PEOPLE ARE KILLED.
1993 THE BRADY BILL, LEGISLATING GUN CONTROL, IS SIGNED INTO LAW.
1995 THE OKLAHOMA CITY BOMBING LEAVES 168 PEOPLE DEAD.

2000

1995 LOUIS FARRAKHAN LEADS THE MILLION MAN MARCH AND RALLY IN WASHINGTON, D.C.
1997 PRINCESS DIANA IS KILLED IN CAR CRASH IN PARIS ON AUGUST 31.
1998 A TERRORIST BOMBS KILL 200 PEOPLE AT U.S. EMBASSIES IN KENYA AND TANZANIA.
1999 TWO STUDENT GUNMEN KILL THIRTEEN STUDENTS AND TEACHERS BEFORE KILLING THEMSELVES AT COLUMBINE HIGH SCHOOL IN COLORADO ON APRIL 20.

2001

2001 ON SEPTEMBER 11, TWO HIJACKED AIRPLANES STRIKE AND DESTROY BOTH TOWERS OF THE WORLD TRADE CENTER, THE WORST ATTACK EVER ON AMERICAN SOIL. A THIRD PLANE STRIKES THE PENTAGON, AND A FOURTH CRASHES IN PENNSYLVANIA.
2001 ENRON FILES FOR BANKRUPTCY.
2001 EXPOSURE TO ANTHRAX IN U.S. MAIL KILLS FIVE PEOPLE.
2001 THE ARTIFICIAL LIVER IS INVENTED.

December 13, 2000 Al Gore offers his concession after Supreme Court ruled against manual recount of Florida's contested votes

September 11, 2001 World Trade Center buildings destroyed in terrorist attack

November 25, 2002 Created new cabinet-level Department of Homeland Security

January 28, 2003 Presented "Case for War" in Iraq in second State of the Union speech

March 19, 2003 Declared war with Iraq

May 28, 2003 Signed $350 billion tax cut, the third-largest in U.S. history

September 2003 Called for revision of Patriot Act

December 8, 2003 Medicare bill signed, covering prescription drugs

December 13, 2003 Saddam Hussein captured

June 28, 2004 American-led coalition handed over limited sovereignty to Iraq

November 2, 2004 Elected to second presidential term

2005 Vladimir Arutyunian threw a hand grenade toward Bush at Freedom Square in Tbilisi, Georgia.

July 19, 2006 Vetoed the Stem Cell Research Enhancement Act

"All of this was brought upon us in a single day, and night fell on a different world."

GEORGE W. BUSH, SEPTEMBER 2001

September 11 was the defining moment for President Bush

☙ 44 ❧
BARACK HUSSEIN OBAMA
(1961–   )
President (2009–   )

Born in Hawaii, son of a Kenyan father and a Caucasian mother from Kansas, Barack Obama grew up amid cultural diversity, a life that helped him learn understanding and empathy for varying points of view.

BIOGRAPHY

Date of birth: August 4, 1961
Place of birth: Honolulu, Hawaii
Father: Barack Hussein Obama Sr. (1936–82)
Mother: Stanley Ann Dunham Obama (1942–95)
Wife: Michelle Robinson (1964–   )
Children: 2
Date of inauguration: January 20, 2009
Age at inauguration: 48
Vice president: Joe Biden
Secretary of state: Hillary Rodham Clinton
Secretary of treasury: Timothy F. Geithner

HIGHLIGHTS

1967 Moved to Indonesia with his mother and stepfather

1971 Enrolled in Punahou School in Honolulu

1983 Received B.A. from Columbia University, where he majored in political science and foreign relations

1985 Moved to Chicago to work with Developing Communities Project

1988 Enrolled in Harvard Law School

1989 Selected as an editor for *Harvard Law Review*

1990 Became first black president of *Harvard Law Review*

October 3, 1992 Married Michelle LaVaughn Robinson

1992–96 Taught constitutional law at University of Chicago Law School

1995 Published *Dreams of My Father*

1996 Elected to Illinois Senate

2004 Elected to U.S. Senate, fifth African American in the U.S. Senate, the third to be popularly elected

---

2008 Became first African American elected president of the United States

"This is our moment. This is our time—to put our people back to work and open doors of opportunity for our kids; to restore prosperity and promote the cause of peace; to reclaim the American dream and reaffirm that fundamental truth—that out of many, we are one; that while we breathe, we hope, and where we are met with cynicism, and doubt, and those who tell us that we can't, we will respond with that timeless creed that sums up the spirit of a people: 'Yes We Can.' Thank you, God bless you, and may God bless the United States of America."

BARACK OBAMA,
ELECTION NIGHT, NOVEMBER 4, 2008

Barack Obama

"There is not a liberal America and a conservative America. There is the United States of America."

BARACK OBAMA,
DEMOCRATIC NATIONAL CONVENTION, 2004

2001

2009

2003 WORLDCOM FILES FOR BANKRUPTCY.

2003 THE IRAQ WAR BEGINS ON MARCH 19.

2003 BIGGEST BLACKOUT EVER HITS NORTH AMERICA ON AUGUST 14.

2004 SPACE SHUTTLE COLUMBIA DISINTEGRATES, KILLING SEVEN ASTRONAUTS ON FEBRUARY 3.

2005 IN AUGUST, HURRICANE KATRINA HITS THE GULF COAST, CAUSING DEVASTATION IN NEW ORLEANS WHEN LEVEES BREAK.

2005 IN SEPTEMBER, JOHN ROBERTS IS CONFIRMED AS CHIEF JUSTICE OF THE UNITED STATES.

2005 THE PRESIDENT ACKNOWLEDGES THE WARRENTLESS ELECTRONIC EAVESDROPPING ON U.S. CITIZENS BY A NATIONAL SECURITY AGENCY PROGRAM.

2006 SAMUEL ALITO IS CONFIRMED AS ASSOCIATE JUSTICE OF SUPREME COURT IN JANUARY.

2006 THE FIRST WORLD BASEBALL CLASSIC IS HELD IN SAN DIEGO, CALIFORNIA.

2006 NORTH KOREA CLAIMS TO HAVE CONDUCTED ITS FIRST-EVER NUCLEAR TEST, BUT THERE REMAINS SOME QUESTION AS TO WHETHER IT WAS AN ACTUAL TEST OR A PARTIALLY FAILED FIZZLE.

Michelle LaVaughn Robinson
❧ OBAMA ❧
(1964–)
First Lady (2009–)

Growing up in a working-class neighborhood on Chicago's South Side, Michelle LaVaughn Robinson learned from her parents that with hard work people could overcome prejudice. Michelle skipped second grade and moved into her school's gifted-and-talented program when she was in sixth grade. Her high school counselor tried to dissuade her when she decided to apply to Princeton University, feeling her grades were not good enough, but she was accepted and graduated with honors. When she chose Harvard Law School, advisers again tried to change her mind, but she persisted and did well. After graduation in 1988, Michelle joined a Chicago law firm, where she met her husband.

BIOGRAPHY
Date of birth: January 17, 1964
Place of birth: Chicago, Illinois
Father: Fraser Robinson
Mother: Marian Shields Robinson
Husband: Barack Hussein Obama
Marriage: October 3, 1992
Children: Malia, Sasha

HIGHLIGHTS
1985 Received B.A. from Princeton University with a major in sociology, minor in African American studies
1988 Earned law degree from Harvard University
1991 Served as assistant to mayor, then assistant commissioner of planning and development for the city of Chicago
October 3, 1992 Married Barack Obama
1993 Became founding director of Chicago leadership training program Public Allies

1996 Became associate dean of student services at University of Chicago
2005 Appointed vice president of community and external affairs at University of Chicago Medical Center

"And as I tuck that little girl and her little sister into bed at night, I think about how one day, they'll have families of their own. And one day, they—and your sons and daughters—will tell their own children about what we did together in this election."

MICHELLE OBAMA
DEMOCRATIC NATIONAL CONVENTION, 2008

Michelle Obama on the campaign trail.

"For the first time in my adult lifetime, I am really proud of my country. And not just because Barack has done well, but because I think people are hungry for change. And I have been desperate to see our country moving in that direction."

MICHELLE OBAMA

"To tell the truth, I was kind of a sissy. If there was any danger of getting into a fight, I always ran."

Harry S. Truman

John Kennedy's brothers used to joke that he was so sickly that a mosquito took a big risk in biting him.

When FDR was five, his father took him to the White House, where he met President Cleveland. "My little man," said Cleveland, "I am making a strange wish for you. It is that you may never be president of the United States."

"If we expect to become great and good men and be respected and esteemed by our friends, we must improve our time when we are young."

Grover Cleveland at age nine

Richard Nixon weighed eleven pounds at birth. At age ten he said to his mother, "I would like to become a lawyer—an honest lawyer, who can't be bought by crooks."

The most traumatic event of Gerald Ford's youth was meeting his biological father for the first time. He saw him only twice in his life.

2009

George Washington

Born in 1732 at the home of his Virginia planter family, George Washington had a rudimentary education—common in colonial America. Good at math, he took up land surveying at age fourteen. Commissioned a lieutenant colonel in 1754, he fought in the first skirmishes of what grew into the French and Indian War.

George Washington at Mount Vernon talking to one of his slaves, 1797.

From 1759 to the outbreak of the American Revolution in 1775, Washington managed his estate at Mount Vernon, which he had inherited from his half brother Lawrence. Washington served in the Virginia House of Burgesses and the Second Continental Congress in Philadelphia. Elected commander in chief of the Continental army in 1775, he and his ill-trained troops embarked upon a war that would last eight grueling years.

Washington was a prime mover in the steps leading to the Constitutional Convention at Philadelphia in 1787. When the new constitution was ratified, he was unanimously elected president.

Washington's wife, Martha, brought to their new position discretion and a warm hospitality developed over fifty-eight years in Virginia society. The Washingtons entertained in formal style in the nation's temporary capitals, New York and Philadelphia.

Washington knew that he would be establishing precedents for the new nation that would last for generations, and so he proceeded cautiously. He started the custom for future presidents to choose and to consult regularly with their cabinet; he set the two-term limit for presidents that lasted until 1940; in disregarding seniority as a qualification for the chief justice, he set the precedent that has allowed later presidents to draw from younger and more diverse judges.

And although he never infringed on the powers granted to Congress, Washington set the pattern that the president leads in deciding foreign policy. When the French Revolution led to a major war between France and England, Washington heard the views of Jefferson, his secretary of state (pro-French), and Hamilton, his secretary of the treasury (pro-British), then insisted upon a neutral course until the United States could grow stronger.

Among other important and lasting customs and laws, Washington initiated:

- oaths of allegiance sworn by government officials;
- Departments of State and Treasury, Office of the Postmaster General, and Attorney General;
- Supreme Court, and circuit and federal district courts;
- first federal census;
- patent and copyright protection;
- presidential succession;
- U.S. Mint;
- naturalization law.

Leaving office at the end of his second term, Washington enjoyed less than three years of retirement at Mount Vernon, dying of a throat infection in December 1799. Historians speculate about whether anyone other than Washington could have held the disparate colonies and the struggling republic together.

John Adams

John Adams was born in Braintree in the Massachusetts Bay Colony in 1735. A Harvard-educated lawyer and a delegate to the First and Second Continental Congresses, he led in the movement for independence.

In 1764 Adams married Abigail Smith, a distant cousin from the prestigious Quincy family. Like other women of the time, Abigail had no formal education, but she read widely and schooled herself in poetry, philosophy, and politics. It was a marriage of the mind and of the heart, lasting for more than half a century.

During the Revolutionary War, Adams served in France and Holland in diplomatic roles, and helped negotiate the Treaty of Paris. From 1785 to 1788, he was minister to Great Britain, returning to be elected vice president under George Washington. Abigail became a good friend to First Lady Martha Washington and helped her with official entertaining, drawing on her experience of courts and society abroad.

In 1797, when he became President, Adams found relations with France had deteriorated. This was partly due to the 1795 treaty between the United States and Great Britain which the French foreign minister, Charles Maurice Talleyrand considered inimical to French interests. French privateers seized U.S. ships, Talleyrand refused to receive Charles Pinkney, the new U.S. commissioner to France, and war seemed imminent. When Adams sent Elbridge Gerry and John Marshall to join Pinkney in an effort to negotiate, Talleyrand demanded, through three agents, a loan for France and a bribe for himself. The commissioners refused. When correspondence about the affair, referring to the French agents as X, Y and Z became public, public outrage erupted. No war was declared, but naval skirmishes continued for the next two years. Eventually the French agreed to negotiations and the Treaty of Morfontaine ended hostilities in 1800. [if there's room, add] In the meantime the Alien and Sedition Acts, prompted in part by French meddling in U.S. matters, had instituted draconian restrictions on citizen criticism of the administration and on foreigners in the United States.

Sending a peace mission to France brought the full fury of the Hamiltonians against Adams. In the campaign of 1800, the Republicans were united and effective, the Federalists badly divided. Nevertheless, Adams polled almost as many electoral votes as Jefferson, who became president.

Washington crossing the Delaware River on his way to victory over the Hessians at Trenton, New Jersey, December 25, 1776.

Marriage of George Washington and Martha Custis, 1759.

John Adams on the presidency: "No man who ever held the office of president would congratulate a friend on obtaining it."

John and Abigail Adams lived in this saltbox house in Braintree, Massachusetts, for most of their lives.

Thomas Jefferson leaving for his inauguration, 1801.

James Madison in his twenties, when he was contributing to Virginia's constitution.

Victory in the battle of Lake Erie, reclaiming the lake for he United States—a crucial triumph in the War of 1812.

James Monroe in the 1820s, still dressed in the old-fashioned clothes of an earlier era.

As first lady in Philadelphia, Abigail had entertained formally, and also managed to do so in the primitive conditions she found at the new capital in Washington in November 1800. The city was wilderness, the president's house far from completion.

The Adamses retired to Quincy in 1801, and for seventeen years enjoyed the companionship that public life had long denied them. Abigail died in 1818. On July 4, 1826, John Adams whispered his last words: "Thomas Jefferson survives." But Jefferson had died at Monticello a few hours earlier.

Thomas Jefferson

Thomas Jefferson was born in 1743 in Albemarle County, Virginia, inheriting land from his father and social standing from his mother. He attended the College of William and Mary, and later studied law.

In 1772 he married a widow, Martha Wayles Skelton, and they lived in his partly constructed mountaintop home, Monticello. Throughout their ten years of marriage, they appear to have been totally devoted. Seven pregnancies weakened Martha, and she died giving birth to her last child. Two of their daughters lived to maturity. Jefferson never remarried.

As a powerful prose stylist and an influential Virginia representative, Jefferson, at thirty-three, was chosen to draft the Declaration of Independence—a brilliant document that is an assertion of fundamental human rights, and America's most succinct statement of its philosophy of government.

Jefferson served as minister to France in 1785, and secretary of state in President Washington's cabinet, resigning in 1793.

When Jefferson became president in 1801, the crisis in France was over. He slashed military expenditures, cut the budget, eliminated a whiskey tax, and reduced the national debt. He sent a naval force to Tripoli, in North Africa, to fight the Barbary pirates who were harassing American ships in the Mediterranean.

In 1803 Jefferson acquired the Louisiana Territory from Napoleon—land comprising fifteen present-day states, from Louisiana to Montana. Even before the Louisiana Purchase, Jefferson had wanted to explore the vast expanse between the Missouri River and the Pacific Ocean. Now with that territory in U.S. hands, he commissioned his private secretary, Meriwether Lewis, and also William Clark to lead the expedition: a two-year, 8,000-mile trek—ascending the Missouri River, crossing the Continental Divide—along the Columbia River to the Pacific.

In 1809 Jefferson retired to Monticello to design and direct the construction of the University of Virginia. After a long and fascinating correspondence with John Adams while both men were in the twilight of their lives, Jefferson died on July 4, 1826. Adams died on the same day, exactly fifty years after the signing of the Declaration of Independence.

James Madison

A native Virginian, well educated in history and law, James Madison helped frame the Virginia constitution in 1776 and, at age twenty-nine, served in the Continental Congress. An emphatic debater at the Constitutional Convention and coauthor of the *Federalist Papers*, Madison earned the title "Father of the Constitution."

In 1794 he married Dolley Payne Todd, a widow with a young son. The marriage, though childless, was happy. "Our hearts understand each other," Dolley said. For half a century, she was the most important woman in the social circles of America.

At the start of Madison's administration in 1809, the United States had a trade embargo with both Britain and France. The next year, Madison urged Congress to pass a law stating that if either country would accept America's neutral rights, he would forbid trade with the other. Napoleon complied, and Madison suspended trade with Britain.

The British seizure of American seamen and cargoes impelled Madison to give in to the war hawks in Congress. On June 1, 1812, he asked for a declaration of war. It began disastrously for America; its forces were unprepared. The British entered Washington and set fire to the White House and the Capitol. But a few notable military victories, climaxed by General Andrew Jackson's triumph at New Orleans, fueled the idea that the War of 1812 had been gloriously successful. With both Britain and America war weary, the Treaty of Ghent ended the conflict in 1814—with neither side the victor.

However, the War of 1812, often called the Second War of Independence, marked the end of American economic dependence on Britain. Domestic industry prospered, and America took its first steps from a largely farming nation to an industrial one.

In retirement at Montpelier, his Virginia estate, Madison spoke out against the issue of states' rights that threatened to shatter the Union. He wrote, "The advice nearest to my heart and deepest in my convictions is that the Union of the States be cherished and perpetuated."

James Monroe

James Monroe was born in Westmoreland County, Virginia, in 1758. As a young man, he attended the College of William and Mary, fought with distinction in the Continental army, and later studied law under Thomas Jefferson.

As a young politician, he was a member of the Virginia Assembly, the Continental Congress, and in 1790 a U.S. senator. As minister to France from 1794 to 1796, he displayed strong sympathies for the French cause; later, he helped negotiate the Louisiana Purchase.

Monroe's wife, Elizabeth, accompanied her husband to France, arriving in Paris in the midst of the French Revolution. She played a dramatic role in saving Lafayette's wife from the guillotine.

In 1817, during his early administration, Monroe undertook a goodwill tour, beginning what was called the "Era of Good Feelings." Unfortunately, these feelings did not last. Beneath the facade of nationalism, there was sectional unrest. The people of the Missouri Territory applied and failed for admission to the Union as a slave state. The Missouri Compromise bill resolved the struggle, naming Missouri a slave state and Maine a free state, and prohibited slavery north and west of Missouri.

In foreign affairs, Monroe responded to the threat that Europe might try to aid Spain in regaining her former Latin American colonies. Not only must Latin America be left alone, Monroe said, but "the American continents . . . are henceforth not to be considered as subjects for future colonization by any European Power." Twenty years after Monroe died, this became known as the Monroe Doctrine, and it remained the cornerstone of American foreign policy for the rest of the nineteenth century.

John Quincy Adams

John Quincy Adams, the son of John Adams, was born in Braintree (now Quincy), Massachusetts, in 1767. He graduated from Harvard College and became a lawyer, and at age twenty-six, he was appointed minister to the Netherlands. While abroad, he met his future wife, Louisa Johnson, born in London to an English mother—our only first lady born outside the United States.

Adams served as senator, minister to Russia, and later, under President Monroe, a gifted secretary of state. He fixed the present U.S.-Canadian border from Minnesota to the Rockies, obtained the territory of Florida from Spain, and helped formulate the Monroe Doctrine.

Elected president in 1824, Adams announced an ambitious national program. He proposed a network of roads and canals to link the country. He also urged Congress to lead in developing the arts and sciences through a national university, to finance scientific expeditions, and to erect an observatory. With little support from Congress or the people, Adams did not achieve his program.

Badly defeated by Andrew Jackson for a second term, Adams returned to Massachusetts. Unexpectedly, in 1830, he was elected to the House of Representatives, and there for the rest of his life he served as a powerful leader.

Andrew Jackson

Born in a frontier log cabin in the Carolinas in 1767, Andrew Jackson received a meager education. In his late teens he studied law; in his spare time he gambled, drank, chased women, and took dancing lessons. Fiercely jealous of his honor, he killed a man in a duel over an unjustified slur about his wife, Rachel. (Rachel died in 1828, just as she and the president-elect were preparing for his inauguration.)

Jackson was the first man elected from Tennessee to the House of Representatives; then he served briefly in the Senate. A major general in the War of 1812, Jackson became a national hero when he defeated the British at New Orleans.

Jackson defeated Adams for the presidency in 1828, and was elected to a second term in 1832. Like George Washington, Jackson combined the art of a seasoned politician with the decision-making ability of a successful general. Unlike his predecessors, Jackson did not defer to Congress in policymaking but used the power of his veto and his party to command.

The greatest party battle concerned what Jackson called "the Monster"—the Bank of the United States, virtually a government-sponsored monopoly. Jackson opposed it and the American voters backed him.

Jackson was a firm believer in preserving the Union, and there was no serious talk of secession during his administration. He pledged to reduce the national debt, and in 1835 he did so, the first time in the nation's history.

At seventy-eight, "Old Hickory" died at the Hermitage, his home in Nashville. His last words to the members of his household were, "I hope to see you all in Heaven, both white and black, both white and black."

Martin Van Buren

Martin Van Buren was born of Dutch descent to the son of a tavern keeper and farmer, in Kinderhook, New York, in 1782. His formal education ended at age fourteen when he became a legal apprentice.

In 1807 he married his childhood sweetheart, Hannah Hoes. She died of tuberculosis just ten years later.

In a span of twelve years, Van Buren served as senator, governor of New York, secretary of state, vice president, and president. Just two months after his inauguration, in 1837, hundreds of banks and businesses failed. Thousands lost their lands—the worst depression in the country's history to that date. Van Buren's support was ruined, even though he was not responsible for the crisis.

When Texas applied for statehood, Van Buren opposed it, believing it would expand slavery and lead to war with Mexico.

Van Buren was defeated for a second term and again as a candidate for president in 1848. He died at age seventy-nine at Lindenwald, his New York home.

The ailing seventy-eight-year-old Andrew Jackson on April 15, 1845.

John Quincy Adams said, "I am a man of reserved, cold, austere, and forbidding manners . . ."

After his inaugural, Andrew Jackson threw open the White House to the public, which quickly degenerated into a rout.

A contemporary caricature of Martin Van Buren as an opossum.

William Henry Harrison

Born into the Virginia planter aristocracy, William Henry Harrison studied classics and history at Hampden-Sydney College, then studied medicine under Dr. Benjamin Rush in Philadelphia.

In 1791 Harrison embarked on a military and political career that included service in the Indian wars and the War of 1812, appointment as governor of the Indiana Territory, election as U.S. representative and U.S. senator.

Harrison was elected president in 1840. But before he had been in office a month, he caught a cold that developed into pneumonia. On April 4, 1841, he died—the first president to die in office, ending the shortest term in American history.

Because of her husband's sudden death, his wife, Anna, never occupied the White House. She outlived him by twenty-three years.

William Henry Harrison died only a month into his presidency, the shortest term in American history.

"His manner was remarkably unaffected. I thought that in his whole carriage he became his station well."
CHARLES DICKENS SPEAKING OF JOHN TYLER, AT THE WHITE HOUSE, 1842

John Tyler

Called "His Accidency" by his opponents, John Tyler was the first vice president to attain the White House by the death of his predecessor. His first presidential decision was his most important. He had himself sworn in immediately, thus paving the way for future orderly transfers of power after the deaths of presidents while in office.

Tyler was born into a prosperous Virginia family in 1790. He graduated from the College of William and Mary, studied law, and served Virginia as representative, governor, and senator.

On domestic issues, he relied heavily on his veto power, resulting in the first impeachment resolution against a president, in 1843. The resolution failed.

Tyler, a states' righter, strengthened the presidency, but he also increased sectional differences that led toward civil war. When the first Southern states seceded, Tyler led a compromise movement. Failing, he worked to create the Southern Confederacy. He died in 1862, never taking his seat in the Confederate House of Representatives.

Tyler's first marriage, to Letitia Christian, lasted twenty-nine years. She died just a year after Tyler became president. His second wife, Julia Gardiner, captivated Washington with glittering White House receptions. Fourteen of his children lived to maturity.

President John Tyler was aboard the frigate Princeton *when an experimental gun exploded. By a stroke of luck he was belowdecks at the time.*

"The Mississippi, so lately the frontier of our country, is now only its center. . . ."
JAMES K. POLK, STATE OF THE UNION MESSAGE, 1848

James K. Polk

James K. Polk was born on a farm in Mecklenburg County, North Carolina, in 1795. Studious and industrious, Polk graduated with honors from the University of North Carolina. As a young lawyer he entered politics, served in the Tennessee legislature, and became a protégé of Andrew Jackson.

In 1824 he married Sarah Childress, a politically astute partner to her husband and a charming though straitlaced first lady. She appeared at the inaugural ball but did not dance.

Speaker of the House, Polk was a chief supporter of Jackson in his attack on the Bank of the United States. He served as Speaker until 1839, leaving to become governor of Tennessee.

In 1844 Jackson, correctly sensing that America favored expansion, urged the choice of a presidential candidate committed to "Manifest Destiny"—the desire to own the continent from coast to coast. Polk, though the dark-horse candidate, won the election.

Even before he could take office, Congress passed a resolution offering annexation to Texas, raising the possibility of war with Mexico. And Polk himself seemed to be risking war with Britain in his stand on the Oregon Territory. He at first would settle for nothing less than the entire region but agreed to a compromise, getting the United States the present states of Washington and Oregon.

Acquisition of the Southwest Territory from Mexico proved far more difficult. To bring pressure, Polk sent General Zachary Taylor to the disputed area on the Rio Grande. To Mexico, this was aggression, and it attacked. Congress declared war and—although outnumbered—American forces won repeated victories and occupied Mexico City. Finally, in 1848, Mexico ceded all or part of modern California, Nevada, Utah, Wyoming, Colorado, Texas, New Mexico, and Arizona.

Polk added more than 500,000 square miles to the nation, but its acquisition began a bitter quarrel between the North and the South over the expansion of slavery.

Leaving office in poor health in March 1849, Polk died three months later.

Zachary Taylor

Born in Virginia in 1784, Zachary Taylor grew up in Kentucky. He was a Southern slave owner at the edge of the western frontier. But Taylor did not defend slavery or Southern sectionalism. Forty years in the army had made him a strong nationalist.

In 1810 Taylor married Margaret Smith, the daughter of a prosperous Maryland planter. For forty years, Margaret accompanied her husband to frontier posts across the country, often helping the sick and wounded. She gave birth to six children, three of whom survived. As first lady, Margaret Taylor took no part in formal social functions, relying on her daughter Betty to act as hostess.

During Taylor's short term as president, from 1849 to 1850, Northerners and Southerners argued whether the new Mexican territories should be opened to slavery. Some Southerners threatened secession. Standing firm, Taylor was prepared to hold the Union together by armed force rather than by compromise.

General Zachary Taylor at the battle of Buena Vista, February 23, 1847.

Taylor laid the cornerstone of the Washington Monument on a blistering day, July 4, 1850. He became ill, and within five days he was dead. After his death, the forces of compromise triumphed temporarily, but war came eleven years later.

Millard Fillmore

Millard Fillmore said, "In the North I was charged with being a pro-slavery man . . . and in the South I was accused of being an abolitionist. But I am neither."

Millard Fillmore was born in the Finger Lakes region of New York in 1800. He worked on his father's farm, attended a one-room school, and at age nineteen fell in love with a redheaded schoolmate, Abigail Powers, who became his wife.

A lawyer, a state and federal legislator, then vice president, Fillmore became president at Zachary Taylor's death in 1850.

The Compromise of 1850 dominated Fillmore's three years in office. A supporter despite his antislavery views, Fillmore signed the bill into law. It provided for:

- admission of California as a free state;
- settlement of the Texas borders;
- territorial status to New Mexico and Utah;
- the Fugitive Slave Act, requiring the government to aid in recovering runaway slaves;
- abolishment of the slave trade in the District of Columbia.

The Compromise favored Southern slave interests and fatally divided Fillmore's supporters; he was denied renomination for a second term. Fillmore lost both his wife and daughter the next year, and later remarried. He died in 1874.

Franklin Pierce

Franklin Pierce was born in Hillsboro, New Hampshire, in 1804. He attended private schools and graduated from Bowdoin College, where he made a lifelong friend, the writer Nathaniel Hawthorne. Pierce studied law, served in the New Hampshire legislature, then went to Washington as a representative and a senator. In 1834 he married Jane Means Appleton.

After serving in the Mexican War, Pierce won the Democratic nomination and the presidency. Two months before he took office, the Pierces saw their eleven-year-old son, Benny, killed in a train accident. The Pierces had already lost two sons in infancy. Pierce was devastated, and his wife did not attend his inauguration or any White House affair for two years.

Pierce became president at a time of apparent tranquillity, but he misjudged his times. Although a New Englander, he ignored the abolitionists. And when he signed the Kansas–Nebraska Act, repealing the Missouri Compromise, he let loose a storm that made slavery a greater national issue than ever before, and hastened the disruption of the Union.

Internationally, Pierce encouraged the expansion of trade. The ports of Japan were opened in 1854 in a treaty negotiated by Commodore Matthew Perry.

Refused the renomination, Pierce returned to New Hampshire, leaving his successor to face the rising storm. He died in 1869.

James Buchanan

James Buchanan was born in a log cabin near Mercersburg, Pennsylvania, in 1791. He graduated from Dickinson College. He was elected five times to the House of Representatives, was minister to Russia, a senator, Polk's secretary of state, and Pierce's minister to Britain.

Taking office as president in 1857, Buchanan presided over a rapidly dividing nation. Like Pierce, a Northern Democrat, he favored Southern interests. He supported Kansas's admission as a slave state, infuriating the North and splitting his party. In 1859 antislavery zealot John Brown was hanged for treason after capturing the federal arsenal at Harpers Ferry in Virginia. During the last months of his term, seven Southern states seceded from the Union, forming the Confederate States of America under Jefferson Davis.

Buchanan, our only president who never married, retired to Pennsylvania in 1861 and died seven years later, leaving his successor to resolve the cataclysm facing the nation.

Abraham Lincoln

Before becoming president, Abraham Lincoln wrote a brief sketch of his life: "I was born February 12, 1809, in Hardin County, Kentucky. My parents were both born in Virginia of undistinguished families. . . . My mother . . . died in my tenth year. . . . My father . . . removed from Kentucky to . . . Indiana in my eighth year. . . . It was a wild region, with many bears and other wild animals. There I grew up. . . . Of course when I came of age I did not know much. Still somehow, I could read, write, and cipher . . . but that was all."

Lincoln said that he had about one year of formal education.

Lincoln worked hard to gain knowledge while farming, splitting rails for fences, and clerking at a store in New Salem, Illinois. He was a captain in the Black Hawk War, studied law, was postmaster, and spent eight years in the Illinois legislature. His law partner said, "His ambition was a little engine that knew no rest."

A popular lithograph of James K. Polk, who said of the presidency, "I am heartily rejoiced that my term is so near its close. I will soon cease to be a servant and will become a sovereign."

Franklin Pierce had a series of mishaps in the Mexican-American War, prompting a political cartoonist to suggest he was more buffoon than soldier.

Buchanan (far right) stands in this 1859 photograph with his cabinet. He wrote to his successor, Lincoln, "If you are as happy, my dear sir, on entering [the White House] as I am in leaving it, you are the happiest man in the country!"

A drawing of Abraham Lincoln making a surprise visit to troops in 1865.

Lincoln's opponent during the Civil War: Jefferson Davis (1808–89), president of the Confederate States of America.

"Fondly do we hope, fervently do we pray, that this mighty scourge of war may speedily pass away. . . . With malice toward none, with charity for all, with firmness in the right, as God gives us to see the right, let us strive on to finish the work we are in, to bind up the nation's wounds, to care for him who shall have borne the battle and for his widow and his orphan, to do all which may achieve and cherish a just and lasting peace among ourselves and with all nations."
ABRAHAM LINCOLN,
SECOND INAUGURAL ADDRESS, 1865

Andrew Johnson's impeachment trial in the Senate, 1868.

U. S. Grant (far right), with wife, Julia, and son, on a visit to a mine in Virginia City, Nevada, in 1879. He bet a dollar she wouldn't go down the mine. He lost.

In 1842 Lincoln married Mary Todd. They had four boys, but only one lived to maturity. Mary was a vivacious young woman, but her later life was filled with tragedy. She had an unpredictable temper, phobias, and periods of paranoia. In 1875 her son had her committed to a mental hospital for several months.

In 1858 Lincoln ran for the Senate against Stephen A. Douglas. Lincoln lost the election, but in debating Douglas he gained a national reputation that brought him the Republican nomination—and election—as president in 1860.

In 1861 eleven Southern states seceded from the Union to form the Confederate States of America. Lincoln thought secession illegal, and was willing to use force to defend the Union. When Confederate troops fired on Fort Sumter in South Carolina, and forced its surrender, he called for 75,000 volunteers. The Civil War had begun.

On January 1, 1863, Lincoln issued the Emancipation Proclamation, freeing slaves in states that had seceded. For many in the North, the war became a moral matter. Lincoln was elected to a second term in 1864 as the Union army seemed to be near victory. Ulysses S. Grant accepted Robert E. Lee's surrender on April 9, 1865, at Appomattox, Virginia.

The Civil War ended slavery in the United States. War casualties on both sides were staggering, an estimated 360,000 for the North and 258,000 for the South.

On April 14, 1865, Lincoln was assassinated by John Wilkes Booth at Ford's Theatre in Washington.

Andrew Johnson

With the assassination of Lincoln, the presidency fell upon Andrew Johnson, a Southern Democrat. Although an honorable man, Johnson was one of the most unfortunate of presidents. Opposing him were the Republicans in Congress who favored a "radical" reconstruction of the South.

Born in Raleigh, North Carolina, in 1808, Johnson grew up in poverty and never attended school. He was apprenticed to a tailor, opened a tailor shop, and at eighteen married Eliza McCardle.

Entering politics, he championed the common man, advocating the Homestead Act to provide a free farm for poor settlers. In 1864 he was nominated for vice president under Lincoln.

Johnson treated the South more as a wayward friend than as a conquered enemy. For that he was vigorously opposed by the radical Republicans in Congress. Overriding Johnson, Congress passed the Civil Rights Act of 1866 and the Fourteenth Amendment, requiring states to grant civil rights and citizenship to blacks as a condition for readmission to the Union.

In 1867 Johnson was impeached for dismissing his secretary of war, who had opposed him. He was tried by the Senate and acquitted by one vote.

In 1875 Tennessee brought Johnson back to the Senate. He died a few months later.

Ulysses S. Grant

President Hayes (who had been a Union major general in the Civil War) at a servicemen's reunion clambake in Rhode Island.

Ulysses S. Grant was born in 1822, to the son of an Ohio tanner. At age seventeen, he won an appointment to West Point and graduated in the middle of his class. He fought in the Mexican War under Zachary Taylor.

At the outbreak of the Civil War, Grant organized volunteers, commanded a regiment, and, by 1862, rose to the rank of major general. After his victories at Shiloh and Vicksburg, Grant was appointed commander of the Union army by President Lincoln.

Elected president in 1868 as a war hero, Grant and his wife, Julia, began what she called "the happiest period" of her life. She entertained lavishly, true to the spirit of the Gilded Age.

As president, however, Grant provided neither vigor nor reform. Although a man of scrupulous honesty, he was welcomed to Washington by unscrupulous politicians. He accepted lavish gifts from admirers and allowed himself to be bribed by speculators. Grant's administration was the first to be marked by major scandals.

At retirement, the Grants made a trip around the world. But in 1884 Grant went bankrupt in a banking swindle, then learned he had cancer. He started writing his memoirs to pay off his debts and provide for his family. In 1885, soon after completing the last page, he died.

Rutherford B. Hayes

Winner of the most fiercely disputed election until the Bush-Gore election in 2000, Rutherford B. Hayes brought dignity, honesty, and moderate reform to the presidency.

Hayes was born in Ohio in 1822. He was educated at Kenyon College and Harvard Law School. He fought in the Civil War with the rank of brevet major general. He was a congressman and governor of Ohio before running for president.

Hayes's election over his Democratic opponent, Samuel J. Tilden, who won the popular vote, depended upon contested electoral votes in three states (Florida was one). An electoral commission decided the contest. The final vote: 185 to 184—just two days before the inauguration date.

President Hayes insisted that his appointments be made on merit, not political loyalty. In 1877 he launched a major civil service reform, barring government workers from political activity.

Hayes pledged protection of the rights of blacks in the South, but also advocated local self-government and the withdrawal of troops.

His wife—First Lady Lucy Hayes, a temperance advocate nicknamed "Lemonade Lucy"—was a popular hostess and one of the best-loved women to preside over the White House.

Hayes had announced in advance that he would serve only one term. He died at his Ohio home in 1893.

James A. Garfield

James Garfield was born in Orange, Ohio, in 1831. He graduated from Williams College in Massachusetts, taught classics, fought as a major general in the Civil War, and served seventeen years in Congress. A Republican, he was elected president in 1880 but was assassinated after just 200 days in office.

Garfield restored prestige to the presidency by attacking political corruption in the New York Customhouse and the award of mail route contracts in the West.

In foreign affairs, Garfield's secretary of state invited all Western hemisphere republics to a conference in Washington in 1882. The conference never took place. On July 2, 1881, in a railroad station, Charles Guiteau shot the president. Garfield lingered near death for weeks. For a few days he seemed to rally, but on September 19, 1881, he died from an infection and internal hemorrhage.

First Lady Lucretia Garfield, her husband's inseparable companion, was herself recovering from illness. During the months the president fought for his life, her grief and devotion won the respect and sympathy of the nation.

Chester A. Arthur

Chester Arthur, although robust-looking, suffered from Bright's disease.

Chester Arthur was born to a Baptist preacher in Fairfield, Vermont, in 1829. He graduated from Union College, taught school, was admitted to the bar, and practiced law in New York City.

As collector of the Port of New York, Arthur was a firm believer in the spoils system. As president, however, he transformed himself into a champion of civil service reform, notably signing the Pendleton Act of 1883.

During Arthur's administration, the first general federal immigration law was enacted. Over his veto, Congress suspended Chinese immigration for ten years.

Suffering from Bright's disease, Arthur ran unsuccessfully for renomination in 1884, and died in 1886. One of his last public acts was the dedication of the Washington Monument.

Grover Cleveland

Grover Cleveland was the only president to leave the White House and return for a second term four years later.

He was born in Caldwell, New Jersey, in 1837, and was raised in upstate New York. At age forty-four, he began a political career that carried him to the White House in three years. Running as a reformer and a Democrat, he was elected mayor of Buffalo and later governor of New York.

In 1886 he married Frances Folsom on her twenty-first birthday, the first president to marry in the White House.

As president, Cleveland was no innovator, but he exemplified honesty. He fought corruption and vetoed favors to special interest groups. He signed the Interstate Commerce Act, the first law establishing federal regulation of the railroads.

His first administration spanned four prosperous years, which continued during Harrison's term. However, after the 1892 election, Cleveland faced a severe economic depression—the Panic of 1893. He lost nearly all his public support, and lost the renomination. He died in 1908.

Benjamin Harrison

Benjamin Harrison was born in 1833 on a farm in North Bend, Ohio. He attended Miami University in Ohio and studied law in Cincinnati. After the Civil War—he was a brigadier general by 1865—Harrison served in the Senate before winning the presidency from Cleveland in 1888.

The most important development of Harrison's term was the continuing growth of the United States. Six new states were admitted, bringing the total to forty-four. In 1890 the western frontier no longer existed—the country was settled from coast to coast.

His wife, Caroline, renovated the White House, started the famous collection of White House china, and raised funds for Johns Hopkins University, while giving elegant receptions and dinners.

Harrison was defeated for a second term by Cleveland, and he died in 1901.

William McKinley

William McKinley was born in Niles, Ohio, in 1843. He attended Allegheny College and was teaching school when the Civil War began. He enlisted in the Union army, and by the end of the war was brevet major of volunteers. He studied law, and won a seat in Congress and the governorship of Ohio as a Republican. In 1871 he married Ida Saxton. His marriage was a devoted though tragic one; both daughters died young, and his wife became a lifelong invalid.

James Garfield with his daughter, Molly, before he became president. He would become the second of four American presidents to be assassinated.

Grover Cleveland—the only president to have had two noncontiguous administrations.

An 1892 cartoon depicting Benjamin Harrison being swamped by his grandfather's (President William Harrison) hat.

President McKinley, just a short time prior to his assassination in Buffalo, New York, September 1901.

Teddy Roosevelt, always an intrepid outdoorsman, with John Muir on Glacier Point in Yosemite Valley, California, c.1906.

William Howard Taft campaigned on a promise to continue Theodore Roosevelt's policies; he would have preferred a seat on the Supreme Court.

Woodrow Wilson, touring the country after World War I.

The Spanish-American War dominated McKinley's administration. Cuban revolt against Spanish rule had escalated, and the American public, siding with the revolutionaries, was pressuring McKinley for a U.S. invasion. In April 1898, he asked Congress for a declaration of war. The United States destroyed the Spanish fleet, seized Manila, and occupied Puerto Rico, later annexing the Philippines, Guam, and Puerto Rico.

McKinley's second term came to a tragic end in September 1901. A deranged anarchist shot him while in Buffalo, New York. He died eight days later.

Theodore Roosevelt

At age forty-two, with McKinley's assassination, Vice President Theodore Roosevelt became the youngest president in the nation's history. He brought new excitement to the office and vigorously led the country toward progressive reforms and strong foreign policy.

Roosevelt was born in New York City in 1858 into a wealthy family, but he struggled against ill health in his youth and became an advocate of the strenuous life. In 1884 his first wife, Alice, and his mother died on the same day. Two years later, he married Edith Carow, with whom he had five children—a fun-loving, rambunctious family.

During the Spanish-American War, Roosevelt, a colonel of the Rough Rider Regiment, led a charge at the battle of San Juan that made his political career. In 1898 Roosevelt was elected governor of New York and in 1900 was nominated as McKinley's running mate on the Republican ticket.

Aware of the need for a shortcut between the Atlantic and Pacific, he proposed the construction of the Panama Canal and encouraged Panama's independence from Colombia. He expanded the Monroe Doctrine, preventing foreign bases in the Caribbean.

In 1906 he won the Nobel Peace Prize for mediating the Russo-Japanese War. He also reached an agreement on immigration with Japan, and sent the fleet on a goodwill tour of the world.

Some of Roosevelt's most important achievements were in conservation. He preserved more than 125 million acres of public land in national forests, established the first wildlife refuge, and fostered large irrigation projects.

Leaving the presidency in 1909, Roosevelt went on an African safari, then reentered politics. In 1912 he ran unsuccessfully for a third term as president.

He died in 1919. He had said, "No man has had a happier life than I have led."

William Howard Taft

Born in 1857 to the son of a distinguished judge, William Taft graduated from Yale, studied law, and made his way to the White House via administrative posts. He was the first governor of the Philippines under McKinley. Roosevelt made him secretary of war, and decided Taft should be his successor.

Taft's administration had many positive accomplishments. Arizona and New Mexico were admitted as states, making forty-eight. Taft prosecuted more than twice the number of antitrust suits Roosevelt had—notably against Rockefeller's Standard Oil Company and the American Tobacco Company. Two constitutional amendments were proposed—providing for an income tax and direct election of senators.

First Lady Helen Herron Taft, widely traveled and politically astute, was an enthusiastic hostess. The Tafts celebrated their silver wedding anniversary at the White House with a glittering evening garden party. She planted the capital's famous Japanese cherry trees around the Tidal Basin.

After leaving office, Taft was named chief justice of the United States, a position he held until just before his death in 1930. To Taft, the appointment was his greatest honor.

Woodrow Wilson

Woodrow Wilson was born in Virginia in 1856 and grew up in Georgia during the Civil War, and during reconstruction in the devastated city of Columbia, South Carolina. After graduation from Princeton and the University of Virginia Law School, Wilson earned his doctorate at Johns Hopkins and started an academic career. He married Ellen Louise Axson in 1885. (She died in 1914.) He was president of Princeton for eight years and then elected governor of New Jersey.

Wilson won the presidency in 1912 on the Democratic ticket, campaigning against both Roosevelt and Taft on a program called the "New Freedom," which stressed individualism and states' rights. In his first term, he maneuvered through Congress the most far-reaching social justice legislation of any president to that time: the Underwood Act; the Federal Reserve Act; the Federal Trade Commission; a law prohibiting child labor; another limiting railroad workers to an eight-hour day. With these successes, and the perception that "he kept us out of war," Wilson won reelection.

In 1917, when German submarines resumed sinking U.S. ships, Wilson concluded that America could not remain neutral in the world war. On April 2, 1917, he asked Congress for a declaration of war.

Wilson enunciated America's war aims—the Fourteen Points, the last of which would establish "a general association of nations . . . affording mutual guarantees . . . to great and small states alike." American troops and supplies poured into Europe, turning the tide of war against Germany.

After the Germans signed the armistice in November 1918, Wilson went to Paris to try to build an enduring peace. He presented to Congress the Versailles Treaty, containing the League of Nations Covenant.

But the election of 1918 had favored the Republicans who opposed the treaty. The president made a national tour to rally support. Exhausted, he suffered a stroke and nearly died. The Versailles Treaty failed in the Senate. Nursed by his second wife, Edith, who assumed many routine presidential duties during her husband's illness, he lived until 1924. Edith lived to ride in President Kennedy's inaugural parade in 1961.

Warren G. Harding

Warren Harding was born near Marion, Ohio, attended Ohio Central College, and became the publisher of a successful newspaper, the *Marion Star*. He served Ohio as a Republican in the state senate and as lieutenant governor, and ran unsuccessfully for governor. In 1914 he was elected to the U.S. Senate. He won the White House by an unprecedented 60 percent of the popular vote, the first man to move directly from the Senate to the presidency.

By 1923 the postwar depression seemed to be giving way to a new surge of prosperity, and Harding enjoyed strong support for his domestic programs. He was the first post–Civil War president to speak in the South for the rights of African Americans. First Lady Florence Harding, a popular hostess, restored gaiety and openness to the White House.

Behind the scenes, however, rumors of scandal began circulating. Like Grant, Harding trusted his political cronies, who betrayed him for their own gain. And after he died in office, in 1923, the Teapot Dome oil-leasing scandal was exposed, along with reports of extramarital affairs.

Calvin Coolidge

In Vermont, early in the morning of August 3, 1923, Calvin Coolidge heard that he was president. His father, a notary public, read him the oath of office. Coolidge signed it and then went back to sleep.

Born in Plymouth, Vermont, in 1872, Coolidge graduated with honors from Amherst College in Massachusetts and entered law and politics. A Republican, he rose from local councilman to governor of Massachusetts to vice president.

At his inauguration as president, he said that the nation had achieved "a state of contentment seldom seen before," and pledged to maintain the status quo. He rapidly became popular. In 1924 he was the beneficiary of what was called "Coolidge prosperity." He believed that the government that governs least, governs best.

Coolidge was both the most witty and taciturn of presidents. Shortly before leaving office in 1929, he gave president-elect Hoover advice on getting rid of talkative visitors: "If you keep dead still, they will run down in three or four minutes." Grace said that when a woman bet she could get at least three words of conversation from him, Coolidge quietly said to her, "You lose."

The Coolidges' younger son died at sixteen, but Grace Coolidge never let her grief interfere with the wit and exuberance she brought to the White House.

By 1929, when the Depression hit, Coolidge was in retirement. He died in 1933, having recently remarked to a friend, "I feel I no longer fit in with these times."

Herbert Hoover

Herbert Hoover was born in an Iowa village in 1874, grew up in Oregon, and graduated from Stanford University as a mining engineer. In 1899 he married his college sweetheart, Lou Henry. The newlyweds moved to China, the first of dozens of homes around the globe until war broke out in 1914.

During and after World War I, Hoover won an international reputation as a humanitarian, heading the organization that became the Commission for Relief in Belgium, later directing war relief in Europe. Lou Hoover, who spoke five languages, helped establish canteens, ambulances, and hospitals in London.

Hoover, a Republican, was elected president in 1928. On October 29, 1929, the stock market collapsed and over the next three years thousands of businesses failed, 9 million Americans lost their savings, and 12 million lost their jobs. Despite Hoover's efforts, the crisis worsened. He became the scapegoat for the Depression and was badly defeated in 1932.

After World War II, Presidents Truman and Eisenhower appointed Hoover to several humanitarian and government commissions. He died at age ninety in New York City.

Franklin Delano Roosevelt

Franklin D. Roosevelt was born in 1882 on his father's estate in Hyde Park, New York—now a national historic site. He graduated from Harvard College and Columbia Law School. In 1905 he married Anna Eleanor Roosevelt, his fifth cousin.

Roosevelt entered public service through politics, as a Democrat. He won election to the New York senate in 1910, and served as assistant secretary of the navy under President Wilson.

In the summer of 1921, when he was thirty-nine, Roosevelt was stricken with poliomyelitis. During three years of painstaking convalescence, he strengthened his upper body but never regained the use of his legs. In 1924 he began one of the most remarkable comebacks in American history when he appeared on crutches to nominate Alfred E. Smith. In 1928 Roosevelt was elected governor of New York.

In 1932, in the midst of the Great Depression, "FDR" was elected president, to the first of four terms. By inauguration day, there were 13 million Americans unemployed, and many banks had failed. In his first months in office, Roosevelt launched the New Deal, a vigorous program of social activism, bringing recovery to business and relief to the unemployed. The Tennessee Valley Authority (TVA), the Works Progress Administration (WPA), and the Social Security Act were among dozens of reforms. To reassure the nation, Roosevelt began his famous radio speeches called "fireside chats." In 1936 he was reelected in a landslide.

Eleanor Roosevelt transformed the role of first lady. Sensitive to the needs of the underprivileged of all creeds,

President Hoover recording a speech into a newfangled "talkie" machine.

Warren Harding prided himself on his showmanship. "I am a man of limited talents, from a small town. I do not seem to grasp that I am president."

Calvin Coolidge was said to have a face that looked as if it had been "weaned on a pickle." He also had a predilection for dressing up.

Faces of grief at FDR's funeral procession.

Truman with Churchill and Stalin. He liked both men.

"Hail the conquering hero." Ike in New York City after victory in Europe, 1945.

races, and nations, she worked tirelessly to improve their lot. She held weekly press conferences, traveled across the country, lectured, gave radio broadcasts, and wrote a daily newspaper column. During World War II, she visited troops around the world, and, after her husband's death, she was the U.S. representative to the United Nations. She was the "First Lady of the World."

Roosevelt pledged that the United States would be a "good neighbor" to other nations in the western hemisphere, respecting their rights, not interfering in their affairs. After France fell and England was attacked in 1940, he began aid to England but stopped short of military involvement.

The Japanese attacked Pearl Harbor on December 7, 1941. The next day Roosevelt asked Congress for a declaration of war. The vote was unanimous. Roosevelt organized the nation's manpower and resources for global war. Under his leadership, homefront Americans went all out for victory.

In February 1945, Roosevelt met with Winston Churchill and Joseph Stalin at Yalta to discuss when the Soviet Union would enter the war against Japan, and postwar occupation of enemy territory. Also agreed to was a conference to meet April 25, 1945, in San Francisco, to establish "a general international organization to maintain peace and security," the United Nations.

By this time, Roosevelt's health was deteriorating, and on April 12, at Warm Springs, Georgia, he died of a cerebral hemorrhage.

Harry S. Truman

Harry S. Truman had just finished presiding over a Senate session when he heard that President Roosevelt was dead. During his few weeks as vice president, Truman had scarcely seen the president and had received no briefing on the development of the atomic bomb or the growing tensions with the Soviet Union. Overnight, these and other wartime problems became Truman's to solve.

Truman was born in Lamar, Missouri, in 1884, and grew up in Independence, Missouri. He went to France during World War I as a captain in the field artillery. Returning, he married Elizabeth "Bess" Wallace, his childhood sweetheart; it was a devoted marriage that lasted fifty-three years.

Active in the Democratic party, Truman was elected a county court judge in 1922 and a U.S. senator in 1934.

As president, Truman made some of the most crucial and controversial decisions in history. Warned that an invasion of Japan would likely take a year and cost the Allies hundreds of thousands of casualties, Truman consulted with advisers and decided to use the atomic bomb. Hiroshima (on August 6) and Nagasaki (on August 9) were nearly obliterated. Five days later Japan surrendered.

Truman led the nation in helping create the United Nations, and in June 1945 the charter was signed.

Truman's domestic policy, known as the Fair Deal, included the expansion of Social Security, a full-employment program, a permanent Fair Employment Practices Act, and public housing and slum clearance.

Dangers and crises marked the foreign scene when Truman campaigned successfully in 1948. The Soviet Union had begun installing Communist regimes in neighboring countries. Truman enunciated the program that bears his name—the Truman Doctrine—pledging to aid all countries threatened by Communist revolution. The Marshall Plan (1948–52), named for his secretary of state, stimulated spectacular economic recovery in war-ravaged western Europe. Truman ordered the Berlin airlift; in 1949 the United States and European allies formed the North Atlantic Treaty Organization (NATO) as an answer to the Soviet threat.

Fear of Communist activity in the United States was whipped to a hysterical pitch when Senator Joseph McCarthy listed names of "card-carrying Communists," later culminating in the Army-McCarthy hearings during Eisenhower's administration.

In June 1950 the Communist government of North Korea attacked South Korea. Truman was faced with what he said was his most difficult decision as president. Within hours, he sent planes and ships to Korea. They were joined by military and materiel from fifteen other member nations, forming a command, the first United Nations military effort. Fighting lasted more than three years.

Deciding not to run again, Truman retired to Independence with Bess, who, unlike Eleanor Roosevelt, had preferred to remain in the background as first lady. Truman died at age eighty-eight, on December 26, 1972.

Dwight D. Eisenhower

Dwight Eisenhower was born in Denison, Texas, in 1890, and brought up in Abilene, Kansas. He excelled in sports, and won an appointment to the U.S. Military Academy at West Point. Stationed in Texas, he met Mamie Geneva Doud, whom he married in 1916.

In his early army career, Eisenhower served under Generals John J. Pershing and Douglas MacArthur. After Pearl Harbor, he was called to Washington for a war plans assignment. He commanded the invasions of North Africa in 1942, and as supreme commander of Allied forces in Europe, directed the cross-channel assault on Normandy on June 6 1944—the greatest amphibious invasion in history.

After the war, he became president of Columbia University and later was appointed supreme commander of NATO.

An adoring public all but forced the presidency upon Eisenhower. He was an authentic American hero. "I Like Ike" was an irresistible slogan, and he won a sweeping victory for the Republicans in 1952. In the White House, the Eisenhowers entertained an unprecedented number of foreign leaders. The first lady's evident pleasure in her role endeared her to her guests and to the public.

Eisenhower went to Korea to revive the stalled peace talks, and, in 1953, a truce brought an armed peace along the border of South Korea. The death of Stalin the same year caused shifts in relations with Russia.

Meanwhile, both Russia and the United States had developed hydrogen bombs. With the threat of destruction hanging over the world, Eisenhower met with the leaders of Britain, France, and Russia in Geneva in 1955, but they were unable to reach agreement on ways to reduce cold war tensions.

In September 1955, Eisenhower suffered a heart attack and was hospitalized for seven weeks. He recovered and was elected for a second term.

In October 1957, a year after the election, Russia startled the world by launching Sputnik, the first man-made space satellite. U.S. prestige suffered, and a debate began about the merits of American education.

In domestic policy, Eisenhower continued the New and Fair Deal programs. *Brown v. Board of Education*, the landmark 1954 Supreme Court decision, had outlawed segregation in public schools. As desegregation began, Eisenhower sent troops into Little Rock, Arkansas, to assure compliance. He also ordered the complete desegregation of the armed forces.

Eisenhower concentrated on maintaining world peace. He developed the "atoms for peace" program and the formation of the International Atomic Energy Agency.

Leaving office in 1961, he prayed for peace "in the goodness of time." The Eisenhowers returned to their home in Gettysburg, Pennsylvania. He died on March 28, 1969.

John Fitzgerald Kennedy

John F. Kennedy (JFK) was born in Brookline, Massachusetts, in 1917, and grew up in Bronxville, New York, and also at the Kennedy summer home in Hyannis Port, Massachusetts. In addition to the usual childhood ailments, he contracted Addison's disease and suffered back pain—conditions that lasted his lifetime. Graduating from Harvard in 1940, he entered the navy. In 1943, when his PT boat was rammed and sunk by a Japanese destroyer, Kennedy, though injured, led the survivors to safety.

After the war, he was elected to Congress as a Democrat, advancing in 1953 to the Senate. He married Jacqueline Bouvier in 1953. In 1955, while recovering from a back operation, he wrote *Profiles in Courage*, which won the Pulitzer Prize in biography.

In 1960 Kennedy was a first-ballot nominee for president, running on a program called the "New Frontier." Millions watched the televised debates with the Republican Richard Nixon. Winning by a narrow margin of popular vote, Kennedy became the youngest elected—and the first Roman Catholic—president.

His beautiful wife and two small children entered the White House, and also the hearts of a nation. Jacqueline Kennedy exhibited beauty, intelligence, and class. She made the White House a museum of American history as well as an elegant family home.

In his inaugural address, Kennedy said, "Ask not what your country can do for you—ask what you can do for your country." He hoped America would resume its mission as the first nation dedicated to the advancement of human rights. The Alliance for Progress provided billions of dollars in aid to Latin America. In 1961 the Peace Corps—the signature success of the New Frontier—brought American idealism to the aid of developing nations. But the hard reality of the Communist challenge remained, and the focus of Kennedy's presidency was on foreign affairs.

In 1961 Kennedy permitted a band of Cuban exiles, armed and trained by the CIA, to invade their homeland at the Bay of Pigs. The attempt to overthrow the regime of Fidel Castro was a failure. The Soviet Union then renewed pressure against West Berlin, erecting a wall between West and East Berlin. Kennedy responded by increasing the U.S. military strength, including new efforts in outer space.

In 1962 the Russians installed nuclear missiles in Cuba, bringing the cold war to a climax. In October, Kennedy ordered a blockade on all offensive weapons bound for Cuba. After six days, while the world waited on the brink of nuclear war, the Russians backed down and agreed to dismantle the missiles.

Believing that both America and Russia had a vital stake in stopping the spread of nuclear weapons, Kennedy led negotiations for the Nuclear Test Ban Treaty in 1963. It was ratified by more than a hundred nations.

John Kennedy was assassinated November 22, 1963, in Dallas, Texas. His charisma, the glitter of "Camelot" on the Potomac, and his death have made JFK as much a phenomenon as a president. Historians disagree on his greatness, and an assessment of both the man and his administration continues today.

Lyndon B. Johnson

Within two hours of Kennedy's death, Lyndon B. Johnson was sworn in as president aboard Air Force One at Dallas's Love Field.

Johnson was born in 1908 in central Texas, near Johnson City, which his family had helped settle. He worked his way through Southwest Texas State Teachers College; he taught poor students of Mexican descent.

In 1937 he won election to the House of Representatives on a New Deal platform, helped by his wife, Claudia "Lady Bird" Taylor Johnson, whom he had married in 1934.

During World War II, Johnson served as a lieutenant commander in the navy, winning a Silver Star. After six terms in the House, he was elected to the Senate in 1948, serving as both minority and majority leader.

As president, Johnson urged the nation to "build a great society, a place where the meaning of man's life matches the marvels of man's labor." Nominated by acclamation in 1964, Johnson won the presidency in his own right with a record popular margin—more than 15 million votes.

JFK, Jackie, Caroline, and John Jr. at Hyannis Port, Massachusetts, August 4, 1962, in a photograph by Cecil Stoughton. Just over a year later, Kennedy would be dead.

"If a free society cannot help the many who are poor, it cannot save the few who are rich."
JOHN F. KENNEDY,
INAUGURAL ADDRESS, JANUARY 20, 1961

President Johnson liked to get up close and personal. The recipient of his attention is Supreme Court appointee Abe Fortas.

Richard Nixon, flanked by his daughter Tricia, announces his resignation on August 9, 1974.

An ebullient Betty Ford dancing on the Cabinet Room table, January 19, 1977.

In his first years in office, Johnson won passage of one of the most extensive legislative platforms in American history—the Great Society program. It provided aid to education, urban renewal, beautification and conservation; established Medicare; and attacked poverty, disease, crime, and delinquency. The Civil Rights Act of 1964 barred discrimination in employment. The Voting Rights Act of 1965, Johnson's proudest achievement, outlawed poll taxes and literacy tests, and promoted voter registration.

Lady Bird Johnson was a prime force behind the beautification of the capital and the nation. And she was active in the war on poverty, especially the Head Start program for preschoolers.

Johnson had less success in foreign affairs. His greatest disaster was the Vietnam conflict. He escalated U.S. involvement, but succeeded only in making it one of America's costliest wars and severely dividing public opinion. In 1967 demonstrators marched on the Pentagon, and men burned their draft cards and fled to Canada or Sweden to avoid arrest. Meanwhile, racial riots broke out. In 1968 the Reverend Martin Luther King Jr. was assassinated; two months later, Senator Robert F. Kennedy was assassinated, changing the Democrats' political prospects.

Deciding not to run for a second term, Johnson retired to the LBJ Ranch in Texas. He died on January 22, 1973, just one day before an agreement to end the fighting in Vietnam.

Richard Milhous Nixon

Richard Nixon was born in Yorba Linda, California, in 1913. He had a brilliant record at Whittier College and Duke University Law School before practicing law. In 1940 he married Thelma Catherine "Pat" Ryan. During World War II, he served as a navy lieutenant commander in the Pacific.

After the war, he was elected to Congress as a Republican, and in 1950 he won a Senate seat. Two years later, Eisenhower chose him for his vice-presidential running mate.

Nominated for president by acclamation in 1960, Nixon lost the election to Kennedy by a narrow margin. In 1962 he ran, again unsuccessfully, for governor of California. In 1968 he again won his party's presidential nomination, and in a stunning political comeback, defeated Vice President Hubert Humphrey.

Nixon's domestic accomplishments as president included consumer product safety, the end of the draft, new anticrime laws, and a broad environmental program. One of the most dramatic events was the first moon landing in 1969 by astronauts Neil Armstrong and Edwin Aldrin on Apollo 11.

Nixon's most important achievements were in his quest for world peace. In a dramatic departure in U.S. foreign policy, Nixon visited China, the first American president to do so. He called it a "journey for peace," easing tensions with China by an agreement to broaden scientific, cultural, and trade contacts. Four months later, he met with Russian leader Leonid Brezhnev and signed the SALT agreement, limiting nuclear weapons.

In his 1972 bid for a second term, Nixon defeated Democrat George McGovern in a landslide election. Three days after his inaugural address, Nixon announced that an agreement with North Vietnam had been reached: American troops would be withdrawn and American prisoners of war released. Involvement in the Vietnam War had cost the United States 58,000 dead, 304,000 wounded, and, according to the Congressional Research Service, $650 billion, in inflation-adjusted figures.

Within a few months, Nixon's administration was besieged by the Watergate scandal—one of the most severe constitutional crises in U.S. history. In 1972 a break-in at the offices of the Democratic National Committee was traced to officials of Nixon's reelection committee. Several administration officials resigned; and some were later convicted of covering up the affair. Nixon denied any personal involvement, but tape recordings indicated he had tried to divert the investigation.

Faced with almost certain impeachment, Nixon resigned the presidency on August 9, 1974. As he spoke, his wife, Pat—perhaps the most dutiful and underrated first lady—stood tearfully beside him. The Nixons retired, settling on the East Coast. In his last years, Nixon regained a measure of public acclaim, especially abroad. He died on April 22, 1994.

Gerald Rudolph Ford

On August 9, 1974, minutes after Nixon resigned, Gerald Ford took the oath of office. He said, "Our long national nightmare is over. Our Constitution works; our great Republic is a government of laws and not of men."

Born in Omaha, Nebraska, in 1913, Ford grew up in Grand Rapids, Michigan. He starred on the University of Michigan football team, was offered a professional contract, but instead went to Yale, where he coached football while earning his law degree. In World War II, he served in the navy in the South Pacific, earning the rank of lieutenant commander. After the war, he served twenty-five years in Congress, eight as minority leader. In 1948 he married Elizabeth "Betty" Bloomer, a popular, outspoken first lady whose candor about her breast cancer and alcoholism won wide respect.

As president, Ford immediately tried to calm controversy by granting Nixon a full pardon. Instead, the pardon aroused scathing criticism that crippled his presidency.

Throughout Ford's administration, the country suffered a severe economic recession. Consumer prices hit record highs, unemployment rose to the highest level since the 1930s, and Ford was unable to push his programs through a Democratic-controlled Congress.

He turned to foreign affairs to buttress U.S. prestige and revive his leadership. On a trip to the Far East in 1974, he visited Japan—a first for an American president—and South Korea, reaffirming U.S. support and friendship. A summit meeting with Soviet leader Brezhnev set new limitations on nuclear weapons. But American prestige sank to a low ebb in 1975 when South Vietnam, Cambodia, and Laos fell to Communist North Vietnam.

Ford won the Republican nomination in 1976 but lost the election to his opponent, Jimmy Carter.

The Fords retired to Rancho Mirage in California near the main campus of the Betty Ford Center. Gerald Ford died on December 26, 2006.

Jimmy Carter

Jimmy Carter was born in 1924 in Plains, Georgia—the first president born in a hospital. He preferred his nickname, Jimmy, to his full name, James Earl Carter Jr. Peanut farming, politics, and devotion to the Baptist faith were mainstays of his upbringing. In 1946 he graduated from the U.S. Naval Academy and married Rosalynn Smith.

After seven years as a naval officer, Carter returned to Plains to take over the peanut farm left by his late father. In 1962 he was elected to the Georgia senate, and in 1970 became governor of Georgia. As a southern governor, Carter stood out by supporting ecology, efficiency in government, and the removal of racial barriers. At the 1976 Democratic convention, he was nominated for president and defeated Ford. Carter was the first man from the "old South" elected president since Zachary Taylor in 1848.

Despite opposition in Congress, Carter had successes in domestic affairs. He dealt with the energy shortage with a new energy bill and a new cabinet-level Department of Energy. He worked to improve the environment with a ban on dumping raw sewage in the ocean. He doubled the size of the national parks and wildlife refuges, adding 104 million acres of Alaskan lands. He created the Department of Education, bolstered Social Security, and appointed a record number of women, African Americans, and Hispanics to government.

Carter's most lasting achievement as president was the Middle East peace treaty that he helped to negotiate between Egypt and Israel at Camp David in 1978. He concluded the Panama Canal Treaty, ceding the Canal Zone to Panama. Building upon the work of his predecessors, he established diplomatic relations with China and completed negotiation of the SALT II nuclear limitation treaty with the Soviet Union. In person and in speeches, he called for human rights around the world.

There were serious setbacks, however. In November 1979, Iranian militants seized the U.S. embassy in Tehran and took more than sixty American hostages. This incident, together with continuing inflation at home, contributed to Carter's defeat in 1980. Iran finally released the hostages, the day Carter left office.

Jimmy Carter's life after leaving the White House has been one of the most extraordinary in history, eclipsing John Adams, Teddy Roosevelt, and William Taft. Today, through the Carter Center, he and Rosalynn, who proved a skillful speaker and hardworking first lady, pursue the same goals—peace, health care, and human rights—by writing, traveling around the globe, building for Habitat for Humanity, and promoting mental health rights.

Ronald Reagan

Ronald Reagan was born in 1911 in Tampico, Illinois. During high school he earned money as a lifeguard, and then worked his way through Eureka College. After graduation, he became a radio sports announcer. A screen test in 1937 won him a contract with Warner Brothers, and during the next two decades he appeared in over fifty films. In World War II, Reagan served in the U.S. Army Air Forces as a captain, but his nearsightedness disqualified him from combat duty.

In 1940 Reagan married actress Jane Wyman; they divorced in 1948. In 1952 he married Nancy Davis.

After serving as president of the Screen Actors Guild, Reagan toured the country as television host of "General Electric Theater," becoming a spokesman for conservatism. In 1966 he was elected governor of California and was reelected in 1970.

Reagan won the Republican presidential nomination in 1980. Voters, troubled by inflation and the year-long confinement of the American hostages in Iran, swept the Republicans into office.

At age sixty-nine, Reagan was the oldest man ever elected president, but his youthful, vigorous appearance belied his age. Shortly after ending his inaugural address, he announced that the 444-day captivity of the Iran hostages had ended. Two months later, he was shot by John W. Hinckley Jr., but quickly recovered. His grace and wit after the near-fatal incident caused his popularity to soar.

Called the "Great Communicator" with the public and Congress, Reagan signed legislation—called "Reaganomics"—to cut taxes and government spending, curb inflation, increase employment, and strengthen national defense. But late in 1981, the country slid into recession; unemployment rose to its highest level since the 1930s, and defense spending brought a large budget deficit.

By 1984 an economic recovery helped Reagan win a second term with a record number of electoral votes. In 1986 Reagan reformed the income tax, lowering tax rates and simplifying the tax code. By the end of his administration, despite the stock panic of 1987, the nation was enjoying its longest recorded period of peacetime prosperity.

In foreign policy, Reagan worked to achieve "peace through strength," helping to end, finally, the cold war. In dramatic meetings with Soviet leader Gorbachev, he negotiated a treaty that would eliminate intermediate-range missiles. In 1985 the West suffered several

"All the signatories of the United Nations Charter have pledged themselves to observe and to respect basic human rights. Thus, no member of the United Nations can claim that mistreatment of its citizens is solely its own business."
JIMMY CARTER, SPEECH TO THE UN

Jimmy and Rosalynn Carter in Mike Peter's 1977 cartoon in the Dayton Daily News.

Ronald Reagan on the presidency: "Since I came to the White House I got two hearing aids, a colon operation, skin cancer, and a prostate operation, and I was shot. The damn thing is, I've never felt better in my life."

"Above all, we must realize that no arsenal, or no weapon in the arsenals of the world, is so formidable as the will and moral courage of free men and women. It is a weapon our adversaries in today's world do not have."
RONALD REAGAN

"I have just repeated word for word the oath taken by George Washington 200 years ago, and the Bible on which I placed my hand is the Bible on which he placed his. It is right that the memory of Washington be with us today, not only because this is our Bicentennial Inauguration, but because Washington remains the Father of our Country. And he would, I think, be gladdened by this day; for today is the concrete expression of a stunning fact: our continuity these 200 years since our government began."

GEORGE HERBERT WALKER BUSH,
INAUGURAL ADDRESS, 1989

The Bush family gathered during the elder Bush's presidency.

attacks of international terrorism—the hijacking of a TWA airliner, the *Achille Lauro* hijacking at sea, and bombings in Vienna, Rome, and Berlin.

The major scandal of the Reagan years was the 1986 Iran-Contra affair. It was revealed that the administration had secretly sold arms to Iran and diverted the proceeds to the Contra forces in Nicaragua.

In January 1989, the Reagans retired to Bel Air, California. President Reagan told the American people in 1994 that he had been diagnosed with the memory-robbing Alzheimer's disease. His "long good-bye," with Nancy at his side, ended with his death on June 5, 2004.

George Herbert Walker Bush

George Bush was born in Milton, Massachusetts, in 1924. He attended Phillips Academy in Andover. On his eighteenth birthday, he enlisted in the navy. The youngest pilot when he received his wings, he flew fifty-eight combat missions during World War II. On one mission he was shot down over the Pacific Ocean and was rescued from his life raft. He was awarded the Distinguished Flying Cross. In 1945 he married Barbara Pierce.

Bush completed his education at Yale University; he was captain of the baseball team and a member of Phi Beta Kappa. After graduating, he embarked on a career in the oil industry in Texas and became active in the Republican Party, serving two terms as a representative to Congress from Houston. After unsuccessful runs for the Senate, he was appointed to a series of positions: ambassador to the United Nations, chairman of the Republican National Committee, chief U.S. liaison in China, and director of the Central Intelligence Agency.

In 1980 Bush lost the nomination for president but was chosen as running mate by Reagan. In 1988 he won the nomination for president and defeated Michael Dukakis in the election.

Immediately Bush faced a sluggish economy and the scandal of the failure of many of the nation's savings and loan institutions. He broke his campaign pledge not to raise taxes, which he later called a "mistake."

In foreign affairs there was dramatic change. Presidents from Truman to Reagan had tried to contain Communism. The payoff came during Bush's term. The Communist empire broke up, and the Berlin Wall fell, ending the cold war.

Bush's greatest crisis came in 1990, when Iraqi President Saddam Hussein invaded Kuwait. Bush rallied the United Nations, the American people, and Congress, and sent 500,000 U.S. troops to join the allied coalition. After weeks of air and missile strikes, the 100-hour ground war—called Operation Desert Storm—overwhelmed the Iraqi army and liberated Kuwait.

Despite Bush's high marks for this military and diplomatic success, voters focused on the weak economy, rising violence in inner cities, and the continued high deficit. In 1992 he lost his bid for a second term to Democrat Bill Clinton.

First Lady Barbara Bush, endearingly unpretentious, captivated the American people. She chose adult literacy as her special cause and today heads the Barbara Bush Foundation for Family Literacy. The Bushes live in Houston, Texas, and in the family summer home in Kennebunkport, Maine.

William Jefferson Clinton

Bill Clinton was born William Jefferson Blythe III in 1946, in Hope, Arkansas, three months after his father died in an accident. When he was four years old, his mother married Roger Clinton, whose name he took when he was fifteen. As a high school delegate to Boys Nation, he met President Kennedy in the White House Rose Garden, an encounter that inspired Clinton to enter into public service.

Clinton graduated from Georgetown University and in 1968 won a Rhodes scholarship to Oxford University in England. He received a law degree from Yale in 1973 and entered politics in Arkansas. In 1975 he married Hillary Rodham, a graduate of Wellesley College and Yale Law School.

Clinton, a Democrat, was elected Arkansas attorney general in 1976; two years later he won the governorship. After losing a second term, he regained the office and served until he defeated incumbent George Bush in the 1992 presidential election.

Clinton outlined an ambitious domestic program to balance the federal budget and lower national debt. He set health care reform as a major priority. But the new administration met conflict and controversy at every turn—the Whitewater affair; the suicide of White House aide Vince Foster; the botched raid on the Branch Davidians in Waco, Texas; the bombing in Oklahoma City; and the defeat of health care reform.

The chairman of the unsuccessful National Health Care Reform was Hillary Rodham Clinton. Undeterred by critics, as first lady she won many admirers for her support for women and children around the world. She became a U.S. senator for New York.

In foreign affairs, President Clinton favored allied coalitions over military missions. He replaced U.S. troops with UN peacekeepers in Somalia and Haiti. And he supported NATO air raids in war-torn Bosnia. He bombed Iraq when Saddam Hussein stopped U.N. weapons inspections. In 1998 Clinton joined the U.S. with NATO forces to oust Yugoslavia's President Milosevic for his offenses against ethnic Albanians in Kosovo. Clinton became a global supporter for an expanded NATO, more open international trade (NAFTA), and a campaign against drug trafficking. Peace in the Middle East, however—a major goal—eluded him.

In 1998, as a result of issues surrounding indiscretions with a White House intern, Clinton was impeached by the House of Representatives. He was tried in the Senate and found not guilty of the charges. He apologized to the nation and continued to have unprecedented approval ratings for his job as president.

On leaving the White House, the Clintons moved to Chappaqua, New York, Senator Hillary Clinton's home base. Bill Clinton keeps an office in New York City. Both have written best-selling memoirs: *My Life* (his) and *Living History* (hers).

George Walker Bush

The son of former President George H. W. Bush, George W. Bush was born in 1946 in New Haven, Connecticut, and grew up in Midland, Texas. After graduating from Yale, he served in the Texas Air National Guard, received an MBA from Harvard, ran unsuccessfully for Congress, and began a career in the oil industry.

In 1989 he purchased the Texas Rangers baseball franchise. In 1994 he was elected governor of Texas and served for eight years.

Bush's run for president against Vice President Al Gore in 2000 ended in the closest and most disputed election in modern U.S. history. The election was decided by the Supreme Court, making Bush the first man in over a century to become president without winning the popular vote.

The terrorist attacks of September 11 changed George Bush's priorities from those of the "compassionate conservative" on which he had run, turning him into a war president, embracing preemptive strikes and regime change in his war on worldwide terrorism.

Bush demanded that Afghanistan's Taliban regime turn over Osama bin Laden, head of Al-Qaeda, but without success. In October 2001, U.S. and coalition forces ousted the Taliban, and three years later, in 2004, Afghanistan held its first free presidential election.

In 2002, in his first State of the Union address, the president labeled Iran, Iraq, and North Korea as "an axis of evil." Focusing on Iraq, the administration took a forceful stand over weapons of mass destruction it believed Iraq held. Despite strong opposition from many European allies, the president demanded Saddam Hussein step down or face invasion. On March 19, 2003, a U.S.-led coalition invaded Iraq. Saddam was captured and jailed, but coalition troops became involved in violent confrontations with Iraqi insurgents in a chaotic occupation.

On the domestic front, Bush signed the No Child Left Behind Act (2002), which the president described as the cornerstone of his administration, and overhauled Medicare in 2003, providing a prescription-drug benefit for the first time.

President Bush authorized deep tax cuts which, combined with the cost of the Iraq war and domestic antiterrorisism efforts (under the umbrella of the Patriot Act, passed in October 2001), produced record levels of budget deficit.

The 2004 election was hardfought, and not without mudslinging, but Bush eventually won both the popular and electoral college votes against Democratic challenger John Kerry.

Barack Hussein Obama

Barack Obama was born in Hawaii but moved to Indonesia for a few years with his mother and stepfather. Young Barack attended a local school but was also tutored by his mother with lessons from an American correspondence course.

Ultimately this was not enough, and he came back to Honolulu to live with his grandparents and attend Punahou Academy. He became acutely aware of differences—not only racial, but also economic and social.

After high school, he spent two years at Occidental College in Los Angeles, and two years at Columbia University in New York City, studying political science and international relations. Finding the business world unsatisfying, Barack decided to work as a community organizer, helping people work for change in their neighborhoods.

Beginning in June 1985, he worked for three years in Chicago with the Developing Communities Project, setting up a tenants' rights organization and tutoring and job-training programs. Deciding he could be more useful with more education, he enrolled in Harvard Law School.

In February 1990, in his second year, he was elected the first African American president of the *Law Review*. He received his JD from Harvard, graduating magna cum laude, in 1991, and returned to Chicago.

In 1996 Barack Obama was elected to the Illinois Senate. In 2004 he was running for the U.S. Senate and was asked to deliver the keynote address for the Democratic National Convention. He won the 2008 election against Republican John McCain— becoming the first African American president elected in the United States.

"All of you know I'm having to become quite an expert in this business of asking for forgiveness. It gets a little easier the more you do it. And if you have a family, an administration, a Congress, and a whole country to ask, you're going to get a lot of practice."
BILL CLINTON, AUGUST 28, 1998

Barack Hussein Obama

"It took a lot of blood, sweat and tears to get to where we are today, but we have just begun. Today we begin in earnest the work of making sure that the world we leave our children is just a little bit better than the one we inhabit today."
BARACK OBAMA

"Before I end my letter, I pray Heaven to bestow the best of Blessings on this House and all that shall hereafter inhabit it. May none but honest and wise Men ever rule under this roof."

JOHN ADAMS TO ABIGAIL,
AS HE BECAME THE FIRST RESIDENT OF THE
WHITE HOUSE ON NOVEMBER 1, 1800

"This house, for example—I was thinking of it as we walked down this hall, and I was comparing it to some of the great houses of the world that I have been in. This isn't the biggest house. Many, and most, in even smaller countries, are much bigger. This isn't the finest house. Many in Europe, particularly, and in China, Asia, have paintings of great, great value, things that we just don't have here and, probably, will never have until we are 1,000 years old or older. But this is the best house. It is the best house, because it has something far more important than numbers of people who serve, far more important than numbers of rooms or how big it is, far more important than numbers of magnificent pieces of art. This house has a great heart, and that heart comes from those who serve."

FROM NIXON'S FAREWELL
TO WHITE HOUSE STAFF, AUGUST 1974

The White House, far right, during the John Adams administration.

Home, office, museum, and historic gathering place—1600 Pennsylvania Avenue is one of the best known buildings in the world. It is certainly the most famous house in America. For more than 200 years, it has been the home of presidents and first families. Once officially known as the president's house, and later as the Executive Mansion, Americans began calling it the "White House" as early as its first coat of whitewash in 1798. Finally, in 1901, President Theodore Roosevelt made that name official.

Pierre L'Enfant updating President George Washington on his plans for the new capital.

1790–91 A site for the new national capital is selected along the Potomac River. President Washington chooses Pierre L'Enfant as the city planner.

1792 James Hoban is selected as architect for the president's house; the cornerstone is laid.

1800 John and Abigail Adams move into the White House; government relocates from Philadelphia to Washington, D.C.

1801 President Jefferson plants a garden and builds a stone wall around the house; a cooking stove replaces the kitchen's open-hearth fireplace.

British troops burning Washington, D.C., August 24, 1814.

The White House after the fire of August 24, 1814.

1814 On August 24, the British burn the White House and Capitol in the War of 1812.

1817 President Monroe moves into the reconstructed White House.

1822 Pennsylvania Avenue is cut on the north side of the President's Park.

1824 The South Portico is constructed; the park north of the White House is named to honor General Lafayette.

1825 John Quincy Adams develops the first flower garden on the White House grounds and plants ornamental trees.

1830 The North Portico is completed.

1833 Running water is piped into the White House for the first time.

1835 First central heating system installed; Andrew Jackson creates the White House orangery and plants the famous Jackson magnolia on the south side of the house.

1848 Gas lamps installed for James K. Polk replace candles and oil lamps; the installation of a second and improved central heating system is completed.

1850 First Lady Abigail Fillmore obtains congressional funds to establish an official library in the White House.

1853 An efficient hot-water-heating system is installed for President Pierce; running hot water is first piped into the second floor bathroom; the White House orangery is expanded into a greenhouse.

1857 The orangery is demolished and a replacement greenhouse is constructed on the west, adjoining the State Floor of the White House.

1866 The first telegraph office is installed in the White House.

1871 President Grant extends the grounds south, and a round pool is built on the south lawn.

1877 The first telephone is installed for President Hayes, using the phone number "1."

1878 Hundreds of trees are planted; the tradition of planting commemorative trees to represent each president and state is begun.

1870s–80s The conservatory is expanded, rambling beside and over the West Wing and providing a spring garden all year long.

1880 The White House staff begins using typewriters; the Ellipse south of the White House is completed.

1881 The White House has its first hydraulic elevator, and crude "air-conditioning" is used.

1891 Electric wiring is installed.

1898 The first electric elevator is installed.

Jerry Smith, one of Mrs Harrison's staff, engaged in the most thorough cleaning the White House had seen for many decades.

1901 The official name of the executive mansion is changed to the "White House."

1902 McKim, Mead & White perform the Theodore Roosevelt Renovation; the conservatory is removed and a new "temporary" Executive Office Building (the West Wing) is erected. Edith Roosevelt plants a colonial garden to the west.

1909 West Wing office building is doubled in size by a southern expansion that includes the first presidential Oval Office; President Taft purchases official automobiles for the White House and converts the stable into a garage.

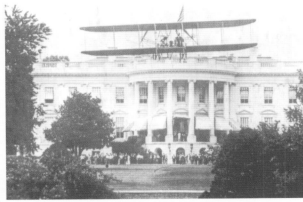

An airplane takes off from the White House lawn in 1911 during the Taft administration.

1913 President Wilson holds the first presidential press conference at the Executive Offices of the White House. Ellen Wilson replaces the colonial garden with a formal rose garden and a new East Garden.

1922 Electric vacuum cleaners are used in the White House for the first time; President Harding has a radio set installed in a bookcase in his study on the second floor.

1925 President Coolidge makes the first national radio broadcast from the White House.

1926 The White House acquires its first electric refrigerator; iceboxes had been in use since the Polk administration.

1933 President Franklin D. Roosevelt begins radio broadcasts, known as fireside chats, to the nation from the White House. A heated indoor swimming pool is built in the west terrace for President Roosevelt's therapy. (The pool was covered in 1974, and the space was converted into a room for press briefings.)

1934 The West Wing is rebuilt and expanded with a new Oval Office and Cabinet Room in an eastern extension.

1942 An East Wing office building is erected, including a bomb shelter; a movie theater is added to the East Terrace.

1947 On October 5, the first presidential address telecast from the White House is delivered by President Truman.

1948 The Truman Renovation begins; four years later the project completely reconstructs the interior of the White House and adds two new underground levels and the Truman Balcony.

1961 President Kennedy has the Rose Garden redesigned to serve presidential functions. Jacqueline Kennedy begins restoration of furniture and works of art.

1964 Lady Bird Johnson has the East Garden completed in honor of Jacqueline Kennedy.

During World War I, President Wilson allowed sheep to graze on the White House lawn.

1993 E-mail is introduced in the White House during the Bush administration.

1994 The first White House Web site is created: http://www.whitehouse.gov/.

1995 In response to the Oklahoma City bombing, the Secret Service closes off Pennsylvania Avenue to vehicular traffic in front of the White House.

2007 The press briefing room is renovated, and now has fiber-optic cables and LCD screens.

The White House kitchen, 1890.

The floral splendor of the East Room in anticipation of a formal dinner during the Theodore Roosevelt administration.

Fireworks at a congressional barbecue at the White House on September 23, 1987, during Ronald Reagan's administration.

"Somewhere out in this audience may even be someone who will one day follow in my footsteps, and preside over the White House as the president's spouse. I wish him well."

—BARBARA BUSH, 1990

Assassinations and Near Misses

The "Zero Years" and Tecumseh's Curse

Some people believe that the curse of American Indian Chief Tecumseh has killed U.S. presidents before the ends of their terms in office, if they were elected in a year that ended with a zero. The first victim of the curse was William Henry Harrison, whose troops killed the famous Shawnee chief during the battle of the Thames near Chatham in 1813.

Harrison, *elected in 1840, died of pneumonia after serving thirty-one days in office.*

Lincoln, *elected in 1860, was assassinated in 1865.*

Garfield, *elected in 1880, was assassinated in 1881.*

McKinley, *elected to a second term in 1900, was assassinated in 1901.*

Harding, *elected in 1920, died of a stroke in office in 1923.*

Roosevelt, *elected to a third term in 1940, died of a cerebral hemorrhage in office in 1945.*

Kennedy, *elected in 1960, was assassinated in 1963.*

Reagan, *elected in 1980, survived an attempted assassination. He seems to have broken the curse.*

Abraham Lincoln

On the morning of April 14, 1865, John Wilkes Booth stopped at Ford's Theatre in Washington, D.C., and heard that President Lincoln was planning to attend the evening performance of *Our American Cousin*. Wilkes, age twenty-seven, an actor and Confederate sympathizer, hated Lincoln and wanted revenge for the South's defeat. His attempt the previous month to kidnap Lincoln had failed. Now, with his coconspirators, Booth saw his chance. He would kill Lincoln at the theater. Two other men would target Vice President Andrew Johnson and Secretary of State William Seward.

Lincoln and his wife, Mary, arrived at Ford's Theatre at 8:30 p.m. Booth arrived about 10 p.m., left his horse in a back alley, and made his way to the presidential box where the Lincolns were sitting. The president's bodyguard had left his post. Booth opened the door to the box and shot Lincoln in the back of the head at close range.

Booth jumped to the stage, hit the floor, and broke his left leg. Flashing his knife, Booth crossed the stage to the back door, mounted his horse, and fled.

Lincoln was taken across the street to a bedroom in the Petersen boardinghouse. The wound was fatal, the bullet having split in two on impact, one piece stopping midbrain, the other lodging near the right eye. Gideon Welles, secretary of the navy, was a witness. "The giant sufferer lay extended diagonally across the bed, which was not long enough for him," he wrote. "He had been stripped of his clothes. His large arms . . . were of a size which one would scarce have expected from his spare appearance. His slow, full respiration lifted the clothes with each breath that he took. His features were calm and striking. . . . The respiration of the president became suspended at intervals, and at last entirely ceased at twenty-two minutes past seven." [Morning of April 15, 1865]

Welles watched Mary Lincoln and her oldest son, Robert, struggle with their sorrow. As Lincoln's life ebbed away, Mary wailed, "Where is my husband?" She begged him to take her with him. Lincoln's body lay in state in fourteen different cities before burial in Springfield, Illinois.

Booth and his accomplices were captured by federal troops on April 26 at Garrett's farm near Port Royal, Virginia. Hiding in a barn, Booth refused to surrender. The barn was set on fire and still he resisted. One of the soldiers claimed that he shot Booth; other reports say Booth killed himself. Booth's coconspirators (the plots against Seward and Johnson had failed) were tried by a military tribunal and found guilty. Some were hanged; some were imprisoned.

James Garfield

On July 2, 1881, President Garfield went to the Baltimore and Potomac railroad station in Washington, D.C., to begin a trip to his twenty-fifth college reunion in Williamstown, Massachusetts. There, Charles J. Guiteau—age thirty-nine, a mentally disturbed man who did not get the job he wanted—shot him. Guiteau had been stalking the president for weeks. One of the bullets grazed Garfield's arm; the other lodged in his back and could not be located. In an attempt to find the bullet, Alexander Graham Bell devised a metal detector, but the metal frame of Garfield's bed confused Bell's device.

The execution of Lincoln's assassins, including Mary Surratt on the far left.

Garfield lived for eleven weeks in increasing pain, suffering the infamous July heat typical of Washington. The first lady, Lucretia Garfield, ordered blocks of ice delivered to the president's bedside; then she, her children, staff, and volunteers took turns waving fans to circulate the air cooled by melting ice. That July, 500,000 pounds of ice were contributed by the public. Several inventors offered their electrical devices, and on July 12, it is said that the world's first "air-conditioning machine" went into action.

Garfield weakened, however, and died in Elberon, New Jersey, on September 19, 1881.

Charles Guiteau pleaded not guilty by reason of insanity, but was convicted and publicly hanged on June 30, 1882.

Garfield's assassination by a disappointed office seeker led to the passage in 1883 of the Pendleton Civil Service Act, which rewards people based on merit rather than patronage.

William McKinley

On September 5, 1901, President McKinley addressed the Pan-American Exposition in Buffalo, New York. The next day, as he stood shaking hands with a long line of well-wishers, Leon Czolgosz, age twenty-eight, a Detroit native, approached with his right hand wrapped in a bandage. As McKinley extended his hand, two shots were fired from a concealed pistol. One bullet was apparently stopped by a button; the second penetrated the president's stomach and lodged in his pancreas. Gripping his chest, McKinley fell back into the arms of a security guard. "My wife—be careful how you tell her—oh, be careful," he said.

Leon Czolgosz shot McKinley with a pistol concealed in a bandaged hand.

McKinley was moved to a hospital for two operations, and he seemed to improve, but then relapsed, and died on September 14. The official cause of death was listed as gangrene of the stomach and pancreas. McKinley was fifty-eight years old.

Czolgosz, an admitted anarchist, was convicted and sentenced to death in the electric chair.

The assassination of McKinley confirmed Americans' fears, already stirred by recent assassinations in Europe linked to anarchists. Congress passed laws to target suspected immigrants, prohibiting their entry into the United States.

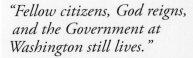

November 1963, President John F. Kennedy's open limousine motorcade in Dallas as shots fired out, hitting both Texas Governor John Connally and the president. Kennedy never regained consciousness. John Connally was seriously wounded but lived to be seventy-six years old. He died in 1993.

A drawing depicting the assassination of President Abraham Lincoln at Ford's Theatre in Washington, D.C., April 14, 1865

Charles Guitean ambushed President Garfield in the Baltimore and Potomac railroad station in Washington, D.C., July 2, 1881.

To John Kennedy, a fatalist with serious chronic illnesses, thoughts of death were not new. On October 28, 1962, at the successful conclusion of the Cuban Missile Crisis, Kennedy joked to his brother Robert, "This is the night I should go to the theater," referring to Lincoln's visit to Ford's Theatre after the Civil War was won.

"We in this country, in this generation, are—by destiny rather than choice—the watchmen on the walls of world freedom. We ask therefore, that we may be worthy of our power and responsibility, that we may exercise our strength with wisdom and restraint, and that we may achieve in our time and for all time the ancient vision of 'peace on earth, good will toward men.' That must be our goal, and the righteousness of our cause must always underlie our strength. Or as was written long ago: 'Except the Lord keep the city, the watchman waketh but in vain.'"

FROM THE SPEECH KENNEDY WAS SCHEDULED TO GIVE AT THE DALLAS TRADE MART, NOVEMBER 22, 1963

John F. Kennedy

In November 1963, President and Mrs. Kennedy traveled to Texas to mend differences between factions in the Democratic Party. On November 22, the Kennedys, with Texas Governor John Connally and his wife, proceeded in an open limousine to the Dallas Trade Mart, where Kennedy was scheduled to speak. The greeting from the crowds lining the streets was warm and enthusiastic. Mrs. Connally said to Kennedy, "You can't say that Dallas doesn't love you."

Moments later, at about 12:30 p.m., as the limousine reached Dealey Plaza, onlookers heard the crack of shots. As the president fell forward, the third shot hit. Jacqueline Kennedy reached for her husband, crying, "Jack! Oh, no! No!" Then she reached out to Secret Service agent Clint Hill, who had already begun to climb over the trunk of the limousine.

A photographer looked up at a building on the corner—the Texas School Book Depository— and caught a glimpse of a rifle barrel being withdrawn from a window on the sixth floor.

Jackie bent low, cradling her husband's head in her lap as the limousine sped to Parkland Hospital. Within minutes, Kennedy and Governor Connally, who had also been hit, were in the emergency room. As doctors frantically tried to save the president, Mrs. Kennedy requested a priest.

Kennedy never regained consciousness. At 1:33 p.m., a press aide announced that he was dead.

His body was flown to Washington, and millions watched his funeral on television three days later. Kennedy was buried in Arlington National Cemetery. An eternal flame marks his grave.

The Dallas police arrested Lee Harvey Oswald, age twenty-four, a former marine and communist sympathizer who worked in the book depository from which the shots apparently were fired. Oswald never made it to trial; two days after the assassination, as Americans watched on television, he was gunned down by Jack Ruby, a nightclub owner.

Possibly no other murder in history has produced as much speculation as Kennedy's assassination. There are many reasons. Presidential assassination, until then unknown in twentieth-century America, conveyed a kind of instant martyrdom. Americans, from the beginning, refused to accept the idea that a lone gunman had murdered the president with no apparent motive. One poll, taken right after the assassination, found that only 29 percent of Americans believed that Oswald had acted alone.

A week after the assassination, President Lyndon Johnson appointed the Warren Commission to investigate. In 1964 the commission concluded that Oswald, acting alone, shot Kennedy; that there was no conspiracy; that Oswald fired three shots, one of which missed the limousine entirely.

In 1979 the House of Representatives issued a report that Kennedy probably was killed as a result of a conspiracy, and that four shots, not three, were fired.

Conspiracy theories continue to circulate. Polls taken in 2003, on the fortieth anniversary of Kennedy's death, indicate that most Americans still believe there was a conspiracy.

George Washington

In 1776, during the Revolutionary War, a conspiracy was uncovered to kidnap and murder General Washington. The plot involved the mayor and governor of New York and a bodyguard, Thomas Hickey, who was publicly hanged on June 28.

Andrew Jackson

In 1835 Richard Lawrence, age thirty-two, approached Jackson as he left the U.S. Capitol and aimed a derringer at close range. The gun misfired. Lawrence drew another gun; it also misfired. Lawrence was found insane and died in an institution.

Abraham Lincoln

In 1861 Lincoln traveled by train to Washington for his inauguration. His guard—Allan Pinkerton, who had founded the Pinkerton National Detective Agency—uncovered a plot to kill Lincoln when he changed trains in Baltimore. Lincoln left in disguise, by special train, and arrived safely in Washington.

Mary Todd Lincoln

Once when returning to the White House after a visit to a friend, Mrs. Lincoln suffered minor head injuries. Some have suggested that the wheel dislodged on her buggy, causing it to overturn. It is thought that the wheel was tampered with.

Theodore Roosevelt

In 1912, again campaigning for the presidency, TR was shot by a psychotic saloon keeper. A bystander deflected the gun; the bullet hit the pocket holding the day's (thick) speech. Not seriously hurt, Roosevelt said, "It takes more than that to kill a Bull Moose."

Franklin Roosevelt

In 1933 Roosevelt had just spoken from his place in a motorcade in Miami, Florida. As the parade was about to proceed, thirty-two-year-old Joseph Zangara fired at the president. Instead, he killed Chicago Mayor Anton Cermak.

Harry Truman

During a renovation of the White House, the Trumans lived across the street. On November 1, 1950, two Puerto Rican nationalists tried to shoot their way into the house, and killed a Secret Service officer. One of the assassins was killed; the other was sentenced to death. Truman reduced the death sentence to life imprisonment, and in 1979 Jimmy Carter granted a pardon.

Gerald Ford

In September 1975, Gerald Ford survived two assassination attempts in California. Lynette Fromme, a cult follower of Charles Manson, attempted to shoot the president in Sacramento, but Secret Service agents disarmed her. Days later in San Francisco, civil rights activist Sara Jane Moore fired at Ford, but a bystander deflected the shot. Both women received life sentences; Moore was released on parole in 2008.

Jimmy Carter

In 1979 as Jimmy Carter was about to speak at a Los Angeles mall, Raymond Lee Harvey was arrested with a pistol. He said he had been hired to create a diversion so Mexican hit men could kill Carter.

Ronald Reagan

John W. Hinckley Jr., age twenty-five, shot Ronald Reagan outside a Washington, D.C., hotel on March 30, 1981. The bullet entered his chest, narrowly missing his heart. Reagan survived. Hinckley was found not guilty by reason of insanity and was committed to St. Elizabeth's, a mental institution in Washington. In December 2003, Hinckley was granted limited home visits under his parents' supervision.

George H. W. Bush

In April 1993, three months after he left office, sixteen suspected terrorists, apparently at the behest of Saddam Hussein, smuggled a car bomb into Kuwait in an attempt to kill George H. W. Bush as he spoke at Kuwait University.

Bill Clinton

On October 29, 1994, Francisco Durran fired shots at the White House from Pennsylvania Avenue. In 1994 Frank Corder crashed his plane on the White House lawn. In 1995 Leland Modjeski climbed over the security fence carrying a gun.

George W. Bush

In May 2005, while George W. Bush spoke at Freedom Square in Tbilisi, Georgia, Vladimir Arutinian threw a live hand grenade at the podium. No one was hurt because a handkerchief wrapped tightly around the grenade didn't allow its firing pin to deploy fast enough.

On January 30, 1835, Andrew Jackson defended himself successfully against would-be assassin Richard Lawrence.

Oscar Collazo lies wounded after his attempt on President Truman's life. Collazo survived.

James Brady and police officer Thomas Delahanty lie wounded after the attempt on Ronald Reagan's life outside the Washington Hilton Hotel, March 30, 1981.

Military Presidents

> *"I do not think there was ever a more wicked war than that waged by the United States against Mexico. I thought so at the time, when I was a youngster, only I had not moral courage enough to resign."*
>
> ULYSSES S. GRANT

Before there were sports legends or movie stars, there were war heroes. Americans have been enchanted by them since the birth of the nation. Historians agree that the importance to political success of having been a soldier changes over time, rising in wartime and declining in peacetime.

Military experience has helped many presidents launch their national political careers. Elections after the Civil War virtually required military service. Hayes and Garfield entered politics from the springboard of their high rank in the Union army. Teddy Roosevelt made a spectacular rise to high office, helped by his heroics at San Juan Hill in the Spanish-American War. Kennedy, Nixon, Ford, and George H. W. Bush pointed with pride to their navy service during World War II. In 2004 the contrast between the military service of John Kerry and George W. Bush exploded into a campaign issue.

Conversely, our history is littered with the unsuccessful presidential dreams of military men. General Winfield Scott (1852), Admiral George Dewey (1900), General Douglas MacArthur (1951), and more recently George McGovern, Alexander Haig, Robert Dole, John McCain, and Wesley Clark—all sought the office and failed.

Six of America's professional soldiers (as against presidents who have had some military experience, like Garfield, Teddy Roosevelt, Truman, Kennedy, etc.)—all generals—did win the White House. All swept into office on a wave of popular enthusiasm.

George Washington

George Washington at the battle of Princeton, January 2, 1777. Painting by John Trumbull (1756–1843).

The young George Washington was consumed with military passion, partly instilled by his beloved halfbrother, Lawrence, who had served as an officer in the Royal Navy. At age twenty George was appointed a major in the Virginia militia during the French and Indian War, but his experiences were not altogether encouraging. On July 4, 1754, he was forced to surrender Fort Necessity to French attackers, and on July 9, 1755, he was with British Major General Edward Braddock at his disastrous defeat at the Monongahela River, although the young Colonel Washington acquitted himself with bravery.

On June 15, 1775, he was unanimously elected commander in chief of the Continental army. During the eight hard years of fighting, he suffered several defeats (for example, New York, Brandywine, Germantown) and experienced only minor victories (at Trenton and Princeton) and one major success as field commander—the last battle of the war, at Yorktown, where Cornwallis surrendered on October 19, 1781. He informed Congress "that a reduction of the British Army under the Command of Lord Cornwallis, is most happily effected."

On the day the British fleet sailed out of New York harbor, Washington met with his officers at Fraunces' Tavern, embraced them, resigned his commission, and left for the comforts of his home in Mount Vernon.

Though Washington did not flaunt his war credentials, his victory for independence led to his unanimous choice in 1789 as America's first president. The Founding Fathers attached the title commander in chief of the armed forces to the presidency.

Andrew Jackson

General Andrew Jackson at the battle of Tallushatchee, November 3, 1813, fought against the Creek Indian allies of the British during the War of 1812.

At thirteen, Andrew Jackson, along with his brother Robert, joined the Continental Army and fought at the battle of Hanging Rock in South Carolina, on August 6, 1780. Jackson's mother and brothers perished in the Revolutionary War.

In 1802 he was elected major general of the Tennessee militia and after victory against the Creeks in March 1814 was made a major general of the U.S. Army. During the War of 1812, he marched to New Orleans, where, on January 8, 1815, he achieved a stunning victory over the British invaders. News spread across the country and Jackson emerged a national hero, leading the crusade for democratic reform. One of his soldiers called him "tough as hickory," and the nickname "Old Hickory" remained with Jackson through his political campaigns.

William Henry Harrison

In 1791 William Henry Harrison gave up his medical studies and joined the Continental army as an ensign. He fought in the Indian wars in the Northwest Territory, and won his first national fame in defeating the Shawnees in the battle of Tippecanoe, November 7, 1811.

In the War of 1812, Major General Harrison defeated a British-Indian force in the battle of the Thames River on October 5, 1813. Two years later the Shawnee chief Tecumseh was killed.

Harrison resigned his commission in 1814 and served in Congress and as minister to Colombia. In the presidential election of 1840, with John Tyler as running mate, he ran successfully against incumbent Martin Van Buren. Harrison's slogan: "Tippecanoe and Tyler Too!"

Zachary Taylor

Zachary Taylor (center) at the battle of Palo Alto, May 8, 1846, an American victory in the Mexican War of 1846–48.

Zachary Taylor—"Old Rough and Ready"—spent forty years in the army, fighting in the War of 1812, the Black Hawk War, and the Second Seminole War. His greatest victories were in the Mexican War, first at Palo Alto and Resaca de la Palma, and then at Monterrey, before defeating General Santa Anna at Buena Vista in 1847. Leaving the army as major general and a war hero, Taylor—who had never held office—ran for the White House on a platform that extolled his military record. He won the election of 1848.

Ulysses S. Grant

Ulysses S. Grant, an 1843 graduate of West Point, fought in the Mexican War (under Zachary Taylor and Winfield Scott) and in the Civil War, retiring as General of the Army—the first commander since Washington to hold that rank.

In 1862 he led the first major Union victory at Forts Henry and Donelson, Tennessee, followed by successes at Shiloh, Vicksburg, Chattanooga, and Richmond. Promoted to commander of all Union armies, Grant defeated the Confederate forces under Robert E. Lee. Lee surrendered to Grant at Appomattox, Virginia, on April 9, 1865.

Grant was the unanimous choice at the 1868 Republican Convention. His acceptance message was, "Let us have peace."

Dwight D. Eisenhower

Dwight D. Eisenhower with—in his description—one of the "coffins on wheels" of the Tank Corps at Fort Meade, 1919.

Dwight D. Eisenhower, also a West Point graduate (1915), rose to five-star general during World War II before becoming president. Like Grant, he had no experience, nor had he held public office.

During World War I, Eisenhower was posted in the United States as an instructor at various military camps. After the war he was assigned to the Panama Canal Zone, later to the Philippines, where he was assistant to General Douglas MacArthur.

Five days after Pearl Harbor, Eisenhower was ordered to report for duty with the War Department. He developed a strategy for opening a "second front," with the invasion of German-occupied France. Gaining a reputation as an organizer, planner, and a man who could reconcile conflicting views, he commanded the successful Allied invasions of French North Africa (1942) and of Sicily and Italy (1943). Named supreme commander of all Allied forces in Europe, he directed the D-day assault on Normandy in June 1944—the greatest amphibian invasion in history.

"To see men without clothes to cover their nakedness, without blankets to lie on, without shoes . . . marching through frost and snow . . . and submitting to it without a murmur, is a mark of patience and obedience which in my opinion can scarce be paralleled."

GEORGE WASHINGTON,
AT VALLEY FORGE, DECEMBER 1777

General Grant (far left) leans over the shoulder of a fellow officer on May 21, 1864, during a rest stop on the way to Richmond.

James Garfield was the youngest major general in the Union army during the Civil War.

Theodore Roosevelt with his Rough Riders after the Battle of San Juan Hill, July 1, 1898.

Presidential Pets

Did you know?

A museum dedicated to the nation's first pets, the Presidential Pet Museum, is located at the President's Park at Williamsburg, Virginia.

A collection of prints and memorabilia is on display. Call 757-259-1121, ext. 107, for information.

William Taft's pet cow, Pauline, in front of the State, War, and Navy building, Washington, D.C., c.1911.

Nearly 400 pets have called 1600 Pennsylvania Avenue home. Whoever makes it to the White House can appreciate the loyal companionship of pets. Running the country can be a hard and lonely job.

George and Martha Washington never lived in the White House, but they had the very first first pets. George was devoted to Nelson, the horse he was riding when he accepted Cornwallis's surrender at Yorktown. But the Washingtons' most famous, or infamous, pet was Martha's parrot. Apparently George and the parrot did not get along, and each kept a close eye on the other.

Birds were popular presidential pets early in our history. Thomas Jefferson had a favorite mockingbird named Curious, which he taught to take food from his lips and to ride on his shoulder.

Dolley Madison owned a green parrot who was said to greet guests, "Constitution, Constitution," which, of course, her husband had helped draft. Dolley was so fond of her parrot that she rescued it—along with a painting and a few pieces of silver—from the burning White House during the War of 1812.

John Quincy Adams owned an alligator given to him by General Lafayette. Adams's wife, Louisa, raised silkworms. Andrew Jackson owned a number of pets, most of which accompanied him to the White House, including his wartime mount, Sam Patches.

Martin Van Buren had two tiger cubs given to him, but they didn't stay very long. William Henry Harrison came with a billy goat and a Durham cow, but they didn't stay long, either, because Harrison himself didn't stay very long. (He died after thirty days in office.)

John Tyler had his favorite horse, named the General. When the General died, Tyler had a grave dug on his estate. He placed a headstone with an affectionate inscription: "Here lie the bones of my old horse, 'General,' who served his master faithfully for twenty-one years, and never made a blunder. Would that his master could say the same! John Tyler."

Warren Harding's Airedales, c.1924.

Zachary Taylor provided a home on the White House grounds for his favorite horse, Old Whitey. Unhappily for Whitey, many White House visitors helped themselves to a few hairs from his tail for souvenirs.

The Lincoln White House was a menagerie of rabbits, turkeys, horses, and goats. The family also had a dog named Fido, and Tad and Willie Lincoln had ponies. Tad also had a white rabbit, goats named Nanny and Nanko, and a turkey named Jack. Jack originally was on the Lincoln's dinner menu, but Tad became fond of the bird and begged his father to spare Jack's life. Lincoln's favorite dog was Jip. Lincoln is also credited with having the first pet cat at the White House.

The very glum Calvin Coolidge with his equally subdued-looking hound.

Herbert Hoover's crazed-looking pet opossum, apprehended by Officer Snodgrass of the White House Police Force, May 6, 1929.

A rare photograph of a wheelchair-bound FDR with his Scottie, Fala, in his lap, Hyde Park, 1941. On the campaign trail in the fall of 1944, FDR complained, "These Republican leaders have not been content with attacks on me, or my wife, or on my sons. No, not content with that, they now include my little dog, Fala. Well, of course, I don't resent attacks . . . but Fala does resent them. . . . His Scotch soul was furious."

Ulysses Grant had a variety of animals. Most were horses. He kept Jeff Davis, a wartime mount, and Cincinnatus, his saddle horse. He also had mares, carriage horses, Shetland ponies, and a racer named Julia. His son Jesse had a parrot, gamecocks, and a Newfoundland dog named Faithful.

Rutherford Hayes kept pedigreed Jersey cows and carriage horses, and a Siamese cat. Scott Hayes, his son, kept dogs and goats.

James Garfield's daughter Molly had a mare named Kit.

Grover Cleveland's wife Frances kept a number of canaries and mockingbirds, as well as a poodle.

Benjamin Harrison's son Russell had a pet goat named His Whiskers. This goat was so ornery that one day the president was forced to chase him down Pennsylvania Avenue when he decided to run away with the Harrison grandchildren.

William McKinley had an Angora cat and a Mexican double-yellow-headed parrot.

But Theodore Roosevelt wins the prize for pet variety. Roosevelt and his six children shared dogs, cats, squirrels, raccoons, bears, lizards, guinea pigs, a hyena, a badger, a blue macaw, chickens, a barn owl, rabbits, a pony, two parrots, a garter snake, a zebra, and a pig named Maude.

William Howard Taft kept a cow named Pauline Wayne. This was the last cow kept at the White House. After that, the White House purchased its milk.

During World War I, Woodrow Wilson kept a flock of sheep at the White House. They kept the grass short, and their wool was sold with the proceeds going to the American Red Cross.

Warren Harding's Airedale, Laddie Boy, was well known nationwide. When Harding died, a song in his dog's honor was written, "Laddie Boy He's Gone."

Calvin Coolidge wins as the president who owned the most unusual pets. Besides dogs, cats, and birds, he had an antelope, a bear, a tiger, lion cubs, and a wallaby.

The most famous presidential dog was Fala, a Scottish terrier beloved of Franklin Roosevelt. The president loved Fala so much that he rarely went anywhere without him. Fala was present when Roosevelt and Winston Churchill signed the Atlantic Charter in 1941 aboard the USS *Augusta*. Fala was also the subject of the first presidential pet biography, a tradition continued by first ladies Barbara Bush and Hillary Clinton.

The Kennedy household included Macaroni the pony, a gift to Caroline from Vice President Lyndon Johnson. Macaroni shared the spotlight with a host of dogs, rabbits, and guinea pigs. Macaroni roamed freely around the White House grounds and received thousands of fan letters from the American public. Caroline also had a dog named Pushinka, who was given to her by the then head of the Soviet Union, Nikita Khrushchev.

Lyndon Johnson created a stir when he picked up his beagles, Him and Her, by the ears.

Checkers, Richard Nixon's cocker spaniel, has a secure place in the history books. In his 1952 "Checkers Speech," Nixon defended his use of a private slush fund by admitting the one gift he intended to keep—the little cocker spaniel that had been given to his daughters.

Barbara Bush provided a birthing room in the White House for the family dog, Millie. In 1990 *Millie's Book* was published, the first "autobiography" by a presidential pet.

The Clinton family dog, Buddy, was a chocolate Labrador retriever who was careful to keep his distance from the Clintons' cat, Socks. Buddy was killed by a car outside his home in New York in 2002.

George W. Bush had a family dog, Barney, a Scottish terrier who was a gift to Laura Bush. In 2005 Barney was joined by another Scottie, Miss Beazley. How the family cat, Willie, feels about this is not known. Springer spaniel Spot, daughter of Barbara Bush's Millie, died in 2004.

Barack Obama's daughters were promised a dog—their first—if their dad won the election. Their main concern during the campaign was what kind and what to name it.

Ten Unusual Presidential Pets

Pygmy hippo: *Calvin Coolidge*

Alligator: *John Quincy Adams*

Elephant: *James Buchanan*

Zebra: *Theodore Roosevelt*

Antelope: *Calvin Coolidge*

Bears: *Thomas Jefferson, Theodore Roosevelt, Calvin Coolidge*

Coyote: *Theodore Roosevelt*

Hyena: *Theodore Roosevelt*

Tigers/lions: *Martin Van Buren, Theodore Roosevelt, Calvin Coolidge*

Wallaby: *Calvin Coolidge*

"If you want a friend in Washington, get a dog."
PRESIDENT HARRY S. TRUMAN

Gerald Ford with his Lab, Liberty, in the Oval Office, November 7, 1974.

Ronald Reagan on presidential helicopter Marine 1 with Lucky, November 1, 1985.

Barbara Bush's dog, Millie, gazing at a painting of Grace Coolidge and her dog, Rob Roy.

Presidential Pastimes

George Washington was an accomplished flutist, as befitted a gentleman of the period.

An 1882 cartoon pokes fun at Chester Arthur's many fishing trips.

How a president fills his rare leisure hours gives us fascinating glimpses into his character. John Quincy Adams liked skinny-dipping in the Potomac River, Teddy Roosevelt was a wrestler, Eisenhower a skilled chef, and Coolidge rode a mechanical horse to keep in shape. And for many people, Jefferson's polymath interests—architecture, botany, meteorology, inventing—are more memorable than the events of his administration.

What presidents do for recreation also reflects the changing customs through our nation's history. For most early presidents—from George Washington to Theodore Roosevelt—the favorite sports were hunting, fishing, and horseback riding. President Taft was the first to take up golf in 1909—and golf has since been the favorite of eleven presidents. Swimming, jogging, skiing, and tennis have also been popular with recent presidents.

Walking, however, wins as the most enduring form of exercise from the early 1800s to today.

Recreational walking began with George Washington, and its devotees included John Adams and his son John Q., Madison, both Harrisons, Coolidge, and Truman, who regularly walked two miles at a fast pace.

Washington was a hunter (foxes), and so were Monroe, Tyler, Hayes, Garfield, Cleveland, and Benjamin Harrison (ducks). Teddy Roosevelt hunted big game in Africa. Lincoln, however, detested hunting.

Lincoln was an avid reader, especially of Shakespeare and the Bible, and could recite whole passages by heart. But perhaps his favorite pastime was swapping jokes with friends.

Presidential fishermen were legion—Van Buren, Pierce, Hayes, Garfield, Arthur, Coolidge, Hoover, Teddy Roosevelt, Eisenhower, Carter, and both the Bushes were all devotees.

Herbert Hoover said, "Fishing is the chance to wash one's soul with pure air. It brings meekness and inspiration, reduces our egotism, soothes our troubles, and shames our wickedness. It is discipline in the equality of men; for all men are equal before fish."

Eisenhower was probably the most serious presidential golfer; it was a bad day if his score reached eighty-five. He had a putting green installed on the grounds. The green is still there, sometimes referred to as the Eisenhower putting green. The best golfer was Kennedy, who typically shot in the upper seventies. Nixon's score was about fifteen strokes higher. Taft, Wilson, Harding, and Coolidge—all golfers as well—didn't like to talk about their scores.

From youth, many presidents were adept sportsmen. For example, Eisenhower played minor league baseball (center field), and football (halfback) at West Point. George Bush Sr. was an All-American in baseball (first base) at Yale. Gerald Ford, a star center at Michigan, was the only president to have been offered National Football League contracts.

Ford was the first president to take to the ski slopes. He had no rival there until Carter succeeded him.

Painting was a hobby of Grant and Eisenhower.

Jefferson was the first president to perform publicly on a musical instrument—the violin. Tyler also played the violin; Truman and Nixon played the piano.

Herbert Hoover once wrote, "The Declaration of Independence is firm that all men (and boys) are endowed with certain inalienable rights . . . which obviously includes the pursuit of fish."

William Taft was a dedicated horseman, although a contemporary once wondered if the horse got as much pleasure carrying the president's formidable 300-plus pounds.

William Taft tried to control his monumental bulk with daily exercise, including golf.

Warren Harding was one in a long line of presidential golfers—although his real love was poker.

Grover Cleveland was a dedicated hunter, seen here in his well-provisioned camp.

Poker-faced Calvin Coolidge (right) working out with less than unrestrained enthusiasm in the Capitol gym.

Teddy Roosevelt was our first tennis-playing president, followed by Taft, Ford, and Carter. Roosevelt tried practically every strenuous sport known in his day—hiking, polo, wrestling, boxing, jujitsu, horseback riding, and swimming in the icy Potomac River.

Some presidents chose less strenuous activities. John Q. Adams was skillful at billiards. He installed a billiard table covered with green felt in the White House. Poker was Harding's game—as well as Truman's and Nixon's. McKinley played euchre and cribbage. Wilson was an avid bridge player. Chess was a diversion for Madison, Lincoln, Garfield, and Hayes, while Bill Clinton did crosswords in ink at championship speed.

As a teenager, Barack Obama dreamed of becoming a professional basketball player.

Ronald Reagan riding on his 688-acre Rancho del Cielo in California's Santa Ynez Mountains.

Presidents in the Making

Teddy Roosevelt, who became a strapping outdoorsman, sportsman, and soldier, was a sickly child. It was his father who encouraged him to develop both his physical and intellectual sides.

William Taft was always on the chunky side. His mother, Louise, wrote, "He is very large of his age and grows fat every day." He would grow up to top 350 pounds.

A child of the American Revolution, John Quincy Adams witnessed the battle of Bunker Hill at eight years of age.

Thirteen-year-old Harry Truman wearing his signature thick-lens eyeglasses. "Without my glasses I was as blind as a bat."

The Log Cabin Myth

An endearing American legend is that anyone can grow up and become president. And for political reasons, many presidents have poor-mouthed their own origins. So the log cabin myth endures. Several presidents born in the 1800s were born in log cabins, yet based on the standards of their day, most of their families ranked as middle class. Even Abraham Lincoln, of log cabin fame, was decidedly middle class at birth—his father was a skilled carpenter as well as a farmer.

The majority have come from wealth and high social standing. The early presidents nearly all attended college. Most were lawyers or generals or both. Early presidents were born when there were perhaps a dozen colleges in the entire nation, and one percent of Americans attended; these facts alone place them in the highest economic tier.

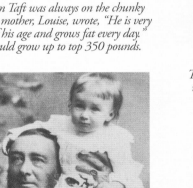

Calvin Coolidge at age three (the only president to be born on the Fourth of July).

The infant FDR on the shoulders of his father, James, in 1883.

Gerald Ford would not learn that he had been adopted until he was in his teens.

"The manner by which women are treated is good criterion to judge of the true state of society. If we knew but this one feature in a character of a nation, we may easily judge the rest."
BENJAMIN HARRISON AT AGE SIXTEEN

Richard Nixon as an infant.

"The largest babe I ever had, he looked like a red Irishman."
JAMES GARFIELD'S MOTHER

Lyndon Johnson, age seven, 1915.

"I haven't liked it since I was a little kid and my mother made me eat it. And I'm president of the United States, and I'm not going to eat any more broccoli!"
GEORGE H. W. BUSH, 1990

The six-year-old Warren Harding with his sisters. His family nickname was "Winnie."

JFK at about eight years old, in a photograph taken around 1925.

Ike in 1907, age seventeen, on a camping trip in Kansas. Born into a poor family, he had to pitch in on family chores: "Scrubbing the floors on Saturday morning . . . washing the dishes, or it could be taking care of the horses or the cows or the chickens."

Presidential Birth States

Presidents born before the United States became independent:
- George Washington
- John Adams
- Thomas Jefferson
- James Madison
- James Monroe
- John Quincy Adams
- Andrew Jackson
- William Henry Harrison

Presidents born in Arkansas:
- Bill Clinton

Presidents born in California:
- Richard Nixon

Presidents born in the Carolinas:
- Andrew Jackson (historians are not sure whether he was born in North or South Carolina)
- James Polk (North Carolina)
- Andrew Johnson (North Carolina)

Presidents born in Connecticut:
- George W. Bush

Presidents born in Georgia:
- Jimmy Carter

Presidents born in Hawaii:
- Barack Obama

Presidents born in Illinois:
- Ronald Reagan

Presidents born in Iowa:
- Herbert Hoover

Presidents born in Kentucky:
- Abraham Lincoln

Presidents born in Massachusetts:
- John Adams
- John Quincy Adams
- John F. Kennedy
- George H. W. Bush

Presidents born in Missouri:
- Harry S. Truman

Presidents born in Nebraska:
- Gerald Ford

Presidents born in New Hampshire:
- Franklin Pierce

Presidents born in New Jersey:
- Grover Cleveland

Presidents born in New York:
- Martin Van Buren
- Millard Fillmore
- Theodore Roosevelt
- Franklin Roosevelt

Presidents born in Ohio:
- Ulysses Grant
- Rutherford Hayes
- James Garfield
- Benjamin Harrison
- William McKinley
- William Taft
- Warren Harding

Presidents born in Pennsylvania:
- James Buchanan

Presidents born in Texas:
- Dwight Eisenhower
- Lyndon B. Johnson

Presidents born in Vermont:
- Chester Arthur
- Calvin Coolidge

Presidents born in Virginia:
- George Washington
- Thomas Jefferson
- James Madison
- James Monroe
- William Henry Harrison
- John Tyler
- Zachary Taylor
- Woodrow Wilson

The Reagan family Christmas card, c.1916. Ronald, age five, is the smaller of the two children, with his brother, Neil, and parents, Jack and Nelle.

Jimmy Carter in his young teens. Like the young George Washington, he would copy out his personal "rules of life."

William Jefferson Blythe III (later William Jefferson Clinton) in 1950, age four.

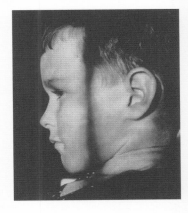

George Bush the elder, age six.

Andrew Johnson did not attend a single day of school. At fourteen he became an indentured servant as apprentice to a tailor.

At age five, Jimmy Carter sold boiled peanuts on the streets of Plains, Georgia. He was free to play with African American children but attended segregated schools.

Firsts, Lasts, and Things of Note

George Washington
- Only president elected unanimously
- Only president inaugurated in New York City
- Shortest inaugural address (second, in Philadelphia)—135 words
- First redhead
- Only president who never lived in Washington, D.C.

John Adams
- First vice president
- First to move into the White House, 1800
- First father of a future president
- Second to die on the Fourth of July
- Longest sentence in an inaugural address—727 words, five times as long as Washington's entire second inaugural address

Thomas Jefferson
- First grandfather (daughter Mary gave birth to first child born in the White House)
- First to be inaugurated in Washington, D.C.
- First to double the size of the nation
- First to shake hands in greeting—Washington and Adams met people with a slight bow
- First to die on 4th of July
- Last redhead to date

James Madison
- First to wear trousers, rather than knee breeches
- Shortest: 5 feet 4 inches
- Lightest: about 100 pounds
- His widow, Dolley, sent the first personal message by Morse telegraph, 1844

James Monroe
- Only president to have a foreign capital named after him—Monrovia, Liberia
- Third to die on the 4th of July
- First father of the bride—daughter Maria's wedding was the first of a president's child in the White House

John Quincy Adams
- First son of a former president
- Only foreign-born first lady (Louisa Johnson was born in England)
- First whose son, John Adams II, was married in the White House
- First published poet

Andrew Jackson
- First use of opinion polls in a presidential campaign
- First target of an assassination attempt
- First to be born in a log cabin
- First to introduce fresh springwater piped in, warm and cold, and shower baths
- First to marry a divorcée
- First to ride on a train

Martin Van Buren
- First president born a U.S. citizen
- Most nicknames: Old Kinderhook—after Kinderhook, New York, his birthplace; from this nickname comes the term "OK."
- First to marry a distant cousin

William Henry Harrison
- First grandfather of a future president
- First to die in office
- Longest inaugural address: 8,445 words, 1 hour and 45 minutes
- Shortest term (thirty-two days)
- Only president who studied medicine
- First president to be photographed in office

John Tyler
- First to become president at predecessor's death
- First whose wife died while in office
- First to marry while in office
- Only president to join the Confederacy
- Fathered the most children: fifteen

James K. Polk
- First to provoke a foreign war
- Greatest territorial expansion—about one-third of what the United States is now
- First to keep all of his campaign promises

Zachary Taylor
- First career army officer
- First Mexican War veteran
- Last to own slaves

Millard Fillmore
- First kitchen stove in the White House
- First born in the nineteenth century
- First library in the White House

Franklin Pierce
- First to be arrested, when he accidentally ran down an elderly woman with his carriage; the charges against him could not be proven and were dropped
- First to put up a Christmas tree in the White House
- Only president to recite his inauguration speech from memory
- Only president to retain his entire cabinet during his term

James Buchanan
- First presidential inauguration to be photographed
- First to send a transatlantic telegram—to Queen Victoria, 1858
- Only bachelor
- Only pet eagle
- Last President to serve in the War of 1812

Abraham Lincoln
- First beard
- First séance in the White House
- Only president to receive a patent—for adjustable buoyant chambers for steamboats
- First to have his portrait on both a coin and paper money
- Tallest: 6 feet 4 inches
- Most future presidents to attend an inauguration—Rutherford B. Hayes, James A. Garfield, Chester Arthur, and Benjamin Harrison attended Lincoln's first inaugural
- First to receive a transcontinental telegram, 1861

Andrew Johnson
- First never to have attended school
- First to be impeached

Ulysses S. Grant
- First Civil War veteran
- African American men were first granted the vote during his administration
- First speeding ticket for riding his horse too fast
- Last former slave owner
- Last Mexican War veteran

Rutherford B. Hayes
- His wife, Lucy, was first to be called "First Lady"
- First Easter egg roll on the White House lawn
- First telephone in White House, 1879
- First to have electricity in White House

James A. Garfield
- First college professor—Hiram College
- First left-handed president
- First American citizen for whom a day of mourning was proclaimed in the royal courts of Europe
- Last born in a log cabin

Chester A. Arthur
- First elevator in the White House
- First "dandy"—nicknamed "Elegant Arthur," he at one time owned eighty pairs of trousers and changed clothes several times a day
- First somnambulist; he enjoyed walking at night and seldom went to bed before 2:00 a.m.
- Only president to destroy all of his personal papers before his death

Grover Cleveland
- Only president to marry in the White House
- Youngest first lady, Frances Folsom, age twenty-one
- First and only first father—daughter Esther, only incumbent's child born in the White House
- Only former hangman, as sheriff of Buffalo, New York

Benjamin Harrison
- First grandson of a former president
- First pet opossum
- First electric lights installed in the White House, 1891
- Last bearded president

William McKinley
- First inauguration recorded by movie camera
- Thought to hold the record for presidential handshaking—2,500 per hour
- Last Civil War veteran
- First to ride in an automobile—after being shot, he was taken to the hospital in a 1901 Columbia electric ambulance

Firsts, Lasts, and Things of Note

Theodore Roosevelt
- Youngest at inauguration—forty-two years, ten months
- Youngest to leave the presidency
- Only Spanish-American War veteran
- First to win Nobel Prize, 1906
- First to travel outside United States while in office—1906, to Panama
- First to fly in an airplane, 1910, in a Wright Brothers plane
- First to publish a book while in office
- First to call the president's house the White House
- First to invite an African American man, Booker T. Washington, to the White House

William Howard Taft
- First to throw out the first pitch on opening day of Major League Baseball
- First presidential car—a model M touring car
- First to play golf
- First presidential funeral broadcast on radio
- First to be buried at Arlington National Cemetery
- Heaviest: more than 300 pounds

Woodrow Wilson
- First Ph.D.— from Johns Hopkins University, 1886
- First university president—Princeton
- First to hold a presidential news conference
- Second president to be a Nobel Prize winner, 1919
- Only president buried in Washington, D.C. (National Cathedral)
- Last to ride to his inauguration in a horse-drawn carriage
- First to cross the Atlantic

Warren G. Harding
- First election results to be broadcast by commercially licensed radio
- First elected with women's votes
- Only newspaper publisher

Calvin Coolidge
- Only president born on the Fourth of July
- First to be sworn in at his family home—Plymouth Notch, Vermont
- First to take naps during administration
- First national Christmas tree lighting ceremony on the White House lawn
- Most press conferences: 520
- First to broadcast a political speech from the White House
- Largest menagerie: a goose, a wallaby, a donkey, a thrush, a lion cub, lots of cats, many dogs, several birds, and a raccoon named Rebecca

Herbert Hoover
- Only Quaker
- First born west of the Mississippi River—West Branch, Iowa
- First high school dropout
- First engineer
- First self-made millionaire
- Only president to speak Chinese

Franklin D. Roosevelt
- Longest time in office
- First to appoint a woman to the cabinet—Secretary of Labor Frances Perkins
- First to appear on television—at the opening of the 1939 World's Fair
- First president named *Time* magazine's "Man of the Year"
- Related by blood or marriage to more former presidents—a total of eleven

Harry S. Truman
- First to speak from the White House on television
- First World War I veteran
- First to pardon the Thanksgiving turkey
- Last not to graduate from college
- Only president to fire a five-star general (MacArthur)

Dwight D. Eisenhower
- First president of all fifty states
- First college football letterman
- First putting green on the White House lawn, 1953
- First licensed pilot
- First to appear on color television
- Last born in nineteenth century
- Only president to serve in both world wars

John F. Kennedy
- First to give a live, televised news conference, 1961
- First navy veteran
- First born in twentieth century
- First Roman Catholic
- Youngest at election
- Youngest at death
- Only president to win Pulitzer Prize—1957 for biography, *Profiles in Courage*
- Only president to be survived by both parents

Lyndon B. Johnson
- First Texan
- First to be sworn in on an airplane
- First to appoint a Afrian American cabinet member
- First to appoint an African American Supreme Court justice

Richard M. Nixon
- First former vice president to become president who did not succeed the president under whom he served
- First election allowing eighteen-year-olds to vote
- First to resign from office
- First to visit all fifty states while in office
- First to visit China
- First to call the moon

Gerald R. Ford
- Only person to hold the office of vice president and president without being elected to either
- Only All-American football player
- First professional male model (*Look* magazine)
- First to pardon a former president
- First to visit Japan
- Only president whose two assassination attempts against him were made by women

Jimmy Carter
- First sworn in using his nickname, Jimmy
- First Annapolis graduate
- First nuclear engineer
- First born in a hospital
- Third president to win Nobel Prize, 2002
- First to light a National Menorah, in Lafayette Park

Ronald Reagan
- Only president to have been a lifeguard
- First movie actor
- First to appoint a woman to the Supreme Court
- Only divorced president
- Oldest at election
- First to survive Tecumseh's curse

George H. W. Bush
- First bomber pilot to be shot down
- First first baseman
- First to host *Saturday Night Live*, October 15, 1994
- First to jump out of an airplane, three times in retirement

Bill Clinton
- First Arkansan
- First Rhodes Scholar
- First woman White House press secretary—Dee Dee Myers
- First woman secretary of state—Madeleine Albright
- First elected president impeached
- First White House Web site

George W. Bush
- First wartime president to seek a tax cut
- First Asian American woman appointed to Cabinet—Elaine Chao
- First to light a Hanukkah menorah at the White House
- First State of the Union webcast
- Fourth to assume the presidency without winning the popular vote
- Most money raised (and spent) in a presidential campaign to date

Barack Obama
- First African American president of the United States
- First African American editor of *Harvard Law Review*
- First president born in Hawaii

Election Year	Presidential Candidates	Electoral Votes
1788	**George Washington**	69
	John Adams	34
	John Jay	9
	Nine others	26
1792	**George Washington**	132
	John Adams	77
	George Clinton	50
	Thomas Jefferson	4
	Aaron Burr	1
1796	**John Adams (Federalist)**	71
	Thomas Jefferson (Democratic-Republican)	68
	Thomas Pinckney (Federalist)	59
	Aaron Burr (Democratic-Republican)	30
	Samuel Adams (Democratic-Republican)	15
	Oliver Ellsworth (Federalist)	11
	Seven others	22
1800	**Thomas Jefferson (Democratic-Republican)**	73*
	Aaron Burr (Democratic-Republican)	73*
	John Adams (Federalist)	65
	Charles C. Pinckney (Federalist)	64
	John Jay (Federalist)	1
1804	**Thomas Jefferson (Democratic-Republican)**	162
	Charles C. Pinckney (Federalist)	14
1808	**James Madison (Democratic-Republican)**	122
	Charles C. Pinckney (Federalist)	47
	George Clinton (Independent-Republican)	6
1812	**James Madison (Democratic-Republican)**	128
	DeWitt Clinton (Fusion)	89
1816	**James Monroe (Democratic-Republican)**	183
	Rufus King (Federalist)	34
1820	**James Monroe (Democratic-Republican)**	231
	John Quincy Adams (Independent-Republican)	1
1824	**John Quincy Adams (Democratic-Republican)**	84*
	Andrew Jackson (Democratic-Republican)	99*
	William H. Crawford (Democratic-Republican)	41
	Henry Clay (Democratic-Republican)	37
1828	**Andrew Jackson (Democratic)**	178
	John Quincy Adams (National Republican)	83
1832	**Andrew Jackson (Democratic)**	219
	Henry Clay (Whig)	49
	John Floyd (Nullifier)	11
	William Wirt (Anti-Masonic)	7

* Because there was no official majority, the House of Representatives decided these elections.

Election Year	Presidential Candidates	Electoral Votes
1836	**Martin Van Buren (Democratic)**	170
	William Henry Harrison (Whig)	73
	Hugh L. White (Whig)	26
	Daniel Webster (Whig)	14
	Willie P. Mangum (Anti-Jacksonian)	11
1840	**William Henry Harrison (Whig)**	234
	Martin Van Buren (Democratic)	60
1844	**James Knox Polk (Democratic)**	170
	Henry Clay (Whig)	105
	James G. Birney (Liberty)	0
1848	**Zachary Taylor (Whig)**	163
	Lewis Cass (Democratic)	127
	Martin Van Buren (Free-Soil)	0
1852	**Franklin Pierce (Democratic)**	254
	Winfield Scott (Whig)	42
	John P. Hale (Free-Soil)	0
1856	**James Buchanan (Democratic)**	174
	John C. Fremont (Republican)	114
	Millard Fillmore (Know-Nothing)	8
1860	**Abraham Lincoln (Republican)**	180
	Stephen Douglas (Democratic)	12
	John C. Breckinridge (Southern Democratic)	72
	John Bell (National Constitutional Union)	39
1864	**Abraham Lincoln (National Union)**	212
	George McClellan (Democratic)	21
1868	**Ulysses S. Grant (Republican)**	214
	Horatio Seymour (Democratic)	80
1872	**Ulysses S. Grant (Republican)**	286
	Horace Greeley (Liberal Republican)	63
1876	**Rutherford B. Hayes (Republican)**	185
	Samuel J. Tilden (Democratic)	184
	Peter Cooper (Greenback)	0
1880	**James A. Garfield (Republican)**	214
	Winfield S. Hancock (Democratic)	155
	James B. Weaver (Greenback)	0
1884	**Grover Cleveland (Democratic)**	219
	James G. Blaine (Republican)	182
	Benjamin F. Butler (Greenback)	0
	John P. St. John (Prohibition)	0
1888	**Benjamin Harrison (Republican)**	233
	Grover Cleveland (Democratic)	168
	Clinton B. Fisk (Prohibition)	0
	Alson J. Street (Union Labor)	0
1892	**Grover Cleveland (Democratic)**	277
	Benjamin Harrison (Republican)	145
	James B. Weaver (Populist)	22

Election Year	Presidential Candidates	Electoral Votes
1896	William McKinley (Republican)	271
	William J. Bryan (Democratic)	176
	John M. Palmer (National Democratic)	0
	Joshua Levering (Prohibition)	0
1900	William McKinley (Republican)	292
	William J. Bryan (Democratic)	155
	John C. Wooley (Prohibition)	0
	Eugene V. Debs (Socialist)	0
1904	Theodore Roosevelt (Republican)	336
	Alton B. Parker (Democratic)	140
	Eugene V. Debs (Socialist)	0
	Silas C. Swallow (Prohibition)	0
1908	William Howard Taft (Republican)	321
	William J. Bryan (Democratic)	162
	Eugene V. Debs (Socialist)	0
	Eugene W. Chafin (Prohibition)	0
1912	Woodrow Wilson (Democratic)	435
	Theodore Roosevelt (Progressive)	88
	William H. Taft (Republican)	8
	Eugene V. Debs (Socialist)	0
1916	Woodrow Wilson (Democratic)	277
	Charles E. Hughes (Republican)	254
	A.L. Benson (Socialist)	0
	J. Frank Hanly (Prohibition)	0
1920	Warren G. Harding (Republican)	404
	James M. Cox (Democratic)	127
	Eugene V. Debs (Socialist)	0
	Parley P. Christensen (Farmer-Labor)	0
1924	Calvin Coolidge (Republican)	382
	John W. Davis (Democratic)	136
	Robert M. La Folette (Progressive)	13
1928	Herbert Hoover (Republican)	444
	Alfred E. Smith (Democratic)	87
	Norman M. Thomas (Socialist)	0
1932	Franklin Delano Roosevelt (Democratic)	472
	Herbert Hoover (Republican)	59
	Norman M. Thomas (Socialist)	0
	William Z. Foster (Communist)	0
1936	Franklin Delano Roosevelt (Democratic)	523
	Alfred M. Landon (Republican)	8
	Willilam Lemke (Union)	0
	Norman M. Thomas (Socialist)	0
1940	Franklin Delano Roosevelt (Democratic)	449
	Wendell L. Wilkie (Republican)	82
	Norman M. Thomas (Socialist)	0
	Roger W. Babson (Prohibition)	0
1944	Franklin Delano Roosevelt (Democratic)	432
	Thomas E. Dewey (Republican)	99
	Norman M. Thomas (Socialist)	0
	Claude A. Watson (Prohibition)	0

Election Year	Presidential Candidates	Electoral Votes
1948	Harry S. Truman (Democratic)	303
	Thomas E. Dewey (Republican)	189
	Strom Thurmond (States' Rights)	39
	Henry Wallace (Progressive)	0
1952	Dwight D. Eisenhower (Republican)	442
	Adlai E. Stevenson (Democratic)	89
	Vincent Hallinan (Progressive)	0
1956	Dwight D. Eisenhower (Republican)	457
	Adlai E. Stevenson (Democratic)	73
	Walter B. Jones (Democratic)	0
1960	John F. Kennedy (Democratic)	303
	Richard M. Nixon (Republican)	219
	Harry F. Byrd (Democratic)	15
1964	Lyndon B. Johnson (Democratic)	486
	Barry M. Goldwater (Republican)	52
1968	Richard Milhous Nixon (Republican)	301
	Hubert H. Humphrey (Democratic)	191
	George Wallace (American Independent)	46
1972	Richard Milhous Nixon (Republican)	520
	George McGovern (Democratic)	17
	John Hospers (Libertarian)	0
1976	Jimmy Carter (Democratic)	297
	Gerald R. Ford (Republican)	240
	Ronald Reagan (Republican)	1
1980	Ronald Reagan (Republican)	489
	Jimmy Carter (Democratic)	49
	John B. Anderson (Independent)	0
1984	Ronald Reagan (Republican)	525
	Walter F. Mondale (Democratic)	13
1988	George Herbert Walker Bush (Republican)	426
	Michael S. Dukakis (Democratic)	112
	Lloyd M. Bentsen Jr. (Democratic)	1
1992	William Jefferson Clinton (Democratic)	370
	George Herbert Walker Bush (Republican)	168
	H. Ross Perot (Independent)	0
1996	William Jefferson Clinton (Democratic)	379
	Robert J. Dole (Republican)	159
	H. Ross Perot (Reform)	0
2000	George W. Bush (Republican)	271
	Al Gore (Democratic)	266
	Ralph Nader (Green)	0
	Patrick Buchanan (Reform)	0
2004	George W. Bush (Republican)	286
	John Kerry (Democratic)	261
	Ralph Nader (Independent)	0
2008	Barack Obama (Democratic)	365
	John McCain (Republican)	173